Thank you!

I so appreciate your willingness to endorse this book. As I bring it into the world, I feel supported by great people.

Endorsements are in the last pages of this book, starting at what would be page 191.

(in alphabetical order)

Judith Blackstone, PhD, Author, *Trauma and the Unbound Body* and *Belonging Here*

Miss Emma Marnie Burchill

Eva Gold, PsyD, Author, *Buddhist Psychology and Gestalt Therapy Integrated: Psychotherapy for the 21st Century*

Steven C. Hayes, PhD, Foundation Professor of Psychology, University of Nevada, Reno. Originator and co-developer of *Acceptance and Commitment Therapy*

Suzanne Noel, Founder, *Recovery Focusing*

Sarah Peyton, Author, *Your Resonant Self: Guided Meditations and Exercises to Engage Your Brain's Capacity for Healing*

Stephen W. Porges, PhD, Distinguished University Scientist, Kinsey Institute, Indiana University Bloomington Professor, Department of Psychiatry, University of North Carolina at Chapel Hill

Mark Schenker, PhD, Author, *A Clinician's Guide to 12-Step Recovery*

Marjorie Schuman, PhD, Author, *Inquiring Deeply: Mindfulness-Informed Relational Psychotherapy and Psychoanalysis*

Inge Sengelmann, LCSW, SEP, RYT, Author, *It's Time to EAT: Embody, Awaken & Transform our Relationship with Food, Body & Self*

Kristen Ulmer, Author, *The Art of Fear*

Jeff Warren, Co-author, *Meditation for Fidgety Skeptics*

Jan Winhall, MSW, FOT, Author, *Treating Trauma and Addiction with the Felt Sense Polyvagal Model*

The Proactive Twelve Steps

A Mindful Program For Lasting Change

All-New Sixth Edition

Serge Prengel

Active Pause®

The Proactive Twelve Steps and a discussion of each step are available
to all at proactive12steps.com

This is the 6th edition of the Proactive Twelve Steps.
The 4th and 5th editions were not published in book form,
just on the website.

Cover photo: Alejandro Barba / Unsplash

Published by Active Pause®
ISBN: 978-1-892482-36-5

Contents

This 6th edition replaces previous editions with all-new contents.

Introduction

We all go through life having an internal view of ourselves and an external view of other people. That is, we are all too aware of the messiness of how we think and feel and do things. But we only see other people from the outside.

What flavor does it have for you? Do you have the sense that you're hopelessly messed up in a way that nobody else could be? Or, maybe, that everybody else is too stupid to notice the complexities of life? It is hard to truly understand yourself and make lasting changes when you keep looking down on yourself or others.

Maybe you have found some kinship in support groups. But, even with these people, you may not feel fully connected. You may feel stuck with an impossible dilemma. Either you're in and lose yourself, or you are yourself and stay an outsider.

How can you find yourself and be yourself amid the pressures of life? How can you make lasting changes that become second nature?

Welcome to the human condition. We all struggle. To paraphrase my friend Jeff Warren, a noted meditation teacher and author: *Being human isn't easy. It takes practice.*

This book is about the practice of being human. It describes a mindful process of self-discovery that leads to lasting change, inspired by the Twelve Steps of A.A.

The big idea

The Twelve Steps of A.A. rest on a powerful idea. When faced with a seemingly intractable problem, you have to give up trying to force change through willpower. The way to solve the intractable problem is to change the structure of your life.

In the original Steps, a considerable role is ascribed to God or to some Higher Power that eventually removes your shortcomings. It is a relief from the burdensome belief that you should be able to control all aspects of your life. But it also implies that healing works in mysterious ways, unknowable to mere mortals.

So it is important to note that the Twelve Steps do not just rely on God or prayer. Most of the steps involve making conscious changes in the way you live and relate to people. Hence the idea to make this healing process more explicit.

A down-to-earth program

I originally wrote the Proactive Twelve Steps for people who, like me, were not part of the Twelve Step culture. Over time, many people in Twelve Step programs have found this approach to be a valuable resource.

My goal was to describe the steps in a down-to-earth way that would make the healing process clearer. The Proactive Twelve Steps describe how we make it possible for change to happen.

This approach makes sense to secular agnostics and atheists as well as religious people. The goal of clarity is not anti-God. You can very much believe in God and still want to know how God's will manifests on an earthly plane. For instance, it is quite possible to believe both in God and modern medicine.

The Proactive 12 Steps are for all people who want to adopt a mindful, proactive approach to change. You can read them on their own or in parallel with the original Steps as a way to gain a new perspective on the process.

What's in this book

The core of this book is Part 1 ("Step by step"), which presents the Proactive Twelve Steps and a discussion of each step. Think of Part 1 as a workbook. That is, something that you work on, not something that you read through. Take time to reflect on each step. See *How to walk the walk* for suggestions on exploring these steps on your own or with others.

We absorb new material more fully when we approach it from different perspectives. So, in addition to the Twelve Steps themselves, this book looks at the process from different angles. I am referring to Parts 2 through 4. You may read these parts sequentially, as you would any other book, or feel free to pick and choose chapters as your curiosity guides you.

Appendix 3, a conversation with neuroscientist Stephen Porges, rounds out this book and is meant to be read last.

Part 1:
Step by step

How to walk the walk

You won't change how you live by just reading a book and nodding in agreement at what it says. You need to make this an active process.

This comment is especially true for Part 1 of this book, which presents the Proactive Twelve Steps and discusses each step. Thus, Part 1 is the core of the process.

I want to encourage you to conduct this exploration in tandem with another person or in a small group. There are many reasons for this.

When people say that the Twelve Steps have helped them, they usually do not mean that they have just read a book about the steps. They credit Twelve Steps meetings and the peer support they provide.

Chances are you've been stewing in your own juices for a long time. It will feel very empowering to realize that other people go through similar struggles.

Speaking to another person gives you a chance to step out of the ruminating mode in which you might too easily fall into when you're on your own.

It also gives you a reason to finish your thoughts, to articulate what you're saying, instead of stopping at half-baked ideas.

This being said, it may not be possible for you to find somebody to share this process with at this point. Or you may not feel comfortable (yet) with this kind of sharing. If so, don't let that stop you from starting the process on your own.

In the rest of this chapter, I will give you some suggestions that apply to both situations, sharing the process with others or doing it on your own.

If you're doing this exploration with a friend or a group, I give you suggestions for doing it in Appendix 2. Essentially, somebody is going to be listening to what you say and summarize what they hear. It gives you a chance to hear yourself think as you listen to what is reflected back to you. And so, you can go further along in your exploration than you would on your own.

Proceeding in this way helps you go deeper. I would not say "digging deeper" because the word "digging" implies a strenuous effort. A more appropriate image would be that of veils lifting. Or the image of layers being peeled off. You have a sense of gentle wonder as the layers are progressively removed, and you keep discovering more stuff.

You see how having somebody listen to you and reflect what they hear can facilitate this deep and gentle discovery process.

How can you have some of that quality if you're on your own? I suggest that you write down your thoughts on each step. Writing, and reading what you wrote, will give you some of the quality of the kind of listening experience that I described above.

When you write things down, you cannot stay at the level of half thoughts. You have to complete your sentences. Thus, writing things down creates more of an incentive for you to go a little deeper. You might stop mid-sentence, and this helps you find the right way to complete it. You probably stop every few sentences to sense what else needs to be said.

Then, when you have written the whole text, you can read it aloud. Listen to it as if you were listening to somebody else. It gives you a chance to hear it as something fresh. You can ask yourself, what did I mean by that? You might change the wording to capture your experience better. Or you might think of something else, something more specific, that goes a bit further than what you first said. Pretty much the way you would if you talked to somebody interested in what you have to say.

Ready to start?

This process is called the Twelve Steps, and there's a reason for it. You take it one step at a time. For instance, take a week for each step before moving on to the next one.

Reflecting on each step is not just a way to better understand what it says. It is a way to practice a reflective, mindful orientation toward your felt experience. This is a quality that you cultivate to be more present in your life. That is, you experience each situation with an ability to feel and think. You notice that there are ways of reacting to it differently from your habitual knee-jerk reactions. You grow from that experience.

In other words: Taking it slowly and mindfully is an integral part of the process. You don't do this by forcing yourself to slow down artificially. You do this by engaging your curiosity. You intentionally prompt your interest by asking yourself a few questions, for instance:

- If I close my eyes, and try to remember the gist of the step, what comes up?

- Does this make sense to me?

- If it makes sense to me, what is it specifically that makes sense?

- If it doesn't make sense to me, what is it that doesn't?

- What situations does it remind me of?

- What is it that I might do differently in these situations, based on my reactions to the step?

- How would it feel inside if I acted this way?

Step 1

I face reality. I am not able to control what I do, and this has serious consequences.

Original wording (AA):

We admitted we were powerless over alcohol—that our lives had become unmanageable.

Discussion of Step 1

So, you have a terrible, horrible, no good, very bad day. And it's not just today. It's been weeks and months, and everything you do seems to make things worse sooner or later. It's like that feeling that kids have when they feel like nothing will ever be right. But you're not a kid. And this is not all in your head, far from that.

Life challenges

There are a lot of genuine difficulties, challenges, problems in your life. It has been dawning on you that it's not just about the external challenges, however tricky they are. It's also how you're responding to them. And so, you know that you must change the way you're responding to things. And you have been trying, but nothing seems to work out, and the consequences are daunting.

It's not good now, and it will get much worse in the future unless something changes dramatically. You have tried to change what you do and found yourself relapsing. Even, in some way, enjoying the relapsing while you were doing it, even though you would deeply regret it afterward.

One way or another, it comes down to the difficulty in controlling your impulses. This is the case with addiction. But it's not necessarily something that people usually describe as an addiction. It could be your tendency to procrastinate or, more generally, be avoidant: this results in a backlog of unresolved issues. Or it could be your tendency to get overly angry. Despite repeated efforts to control your anger, you find yourself erupting in a rage you end up regretting.

You have tried to control your impulses, only to fail so many times. You face a harsh reality: There's a big difference between what you want to do and what you actually do.

Denial

For a long time, you have been in denial. There are many forms of denial: "It's no big deal," or "I don't really have a problem," or "I can handle it," or "I could stop anytime I want," or…

What happens, essentially, is that you don't see what is now blindingly obvious to everybody else. You have a problem. Your life is out of control.

Why have you been in denial? Well, you didn't invent denial. It is a mechanism that is in all of us. It is a coping mechanism that allows us to function under extreme circumstances.

For instance: We are all mortal. It is an inescapable truth that we are all eventually going to die. It is sad and scary. But, if we kept thinking about our death every moment of our existence and feeling sad and scared about that, what kind of life would we have?

So, denial helps us disengage from problems we cannot solve and focus on living in the moment. But there are times when it is not helpful, even harmful. It would be much more effective to take action.

A new beginning

It's not enough to just say: I believe it will work one day if I just keep trying. You need to take action. You need to create a setting in which change is possible and sustainable. This is why you are following a program instead of just improvising as you go along.

At the onset of this program, you are looking squarely at reality. You acknowledge that what you're doing is not working. When you do, you are left with a feeling of emptiness. You don't know what to do or even whether there is a solution. It is terrifying. However, it is this emptiness that allows you to make room for new, unexpected ideas.

Step 1 is a bleak moment in the sense that you are facing the full catastrophe head-on. It is also a new beginning, the first step on a journey to change the structures of your life.

Step 2

I understand that I cannot force change through willpower. I need to disentangle my life patiently.

Original wording (AA):
Came to believe that a power greater than ourselves could restore us to sanity.

Discussion of Step 2

As we left Step 1, things were very bleak, but there was hope for the future. In the Twelve Steps of A.A., hope takes the form of a religious narrative. Out of the depth of despair, there is the possibility of salvation through God. This is exemplified by the song Amazing Grace: "I was lost, and now I'm found."

Where does this leave you if you do not have that kind of religious belief? I suggest you don't take the original Step 2 literally. Instead, pay attention to the big picture, the context in which it is written.

If the Twelve Steps were about being saved by the grace of an all-powerful God, then there would be no need for 12 steps. The instructions would just be: "Trust God, pray, and all sorts of good things will happen."

But there are many more steps than that, and most of them have nothing to do with God. In fact, most of the steps describe a process of making changes in the way you relate to other people and to yourself.

Faith in the process

So why mention God at all if the process itself is actually one that is focused on personal change? Well, it is really hard to start such a process when you are in a state of despair.

Putting Step 2 in context, you see that its role is to give people a reason to believe that change is possible even though circumstances are daunting. The people who started A.A. were Christian. They took for granted the cultural narrative that God is all-powerful and can accomplish miracles. Relating this process to the power of God made it possible to believe in it.

We're now several decades past the time when the Twelve Steps started. We see how millions of people have benefitted from following the Steps. You don't need to believe in God to believe in the process of the Steps. All you need to do is to remember that it has worked for other people.

If you believe in God, by all means, take comfort in the sense that you are in the hand of a benevolent God. If you're an atheist or an agnostic, you don't need to feel like you have to believe in God to undertake this process. What gives you hope and faith is the very existence of the Twelve Steps. They have helped people make changes that feel so impossible that they appear to be nothing short of miraculous.

To be totally clear, the central belief of Step 2 is a belief in the process of the Twelve Steps. It has worked for others and can work for you.

What is the nature of this process?

Let's use a metaphor for this process, what to do with a cord that is all tangled up. How do you disentangle it? If you are impatient and try to pull, all you succeed in doing is getting it even more tangled. The only way to unravel it is to go very slowly. You patiently look for ways to create an opening between strands. And, little by little, you untangle it.

This is the kind of attitude that works for changing deeply ingrained habits. You face the reality that the strands are entangled, and there is no quick and easy way to undo the mess. Then, one by one, you disentangle the various strands of your life.

The stakes are high, as we saw in Step 1. There are serious consequences for yourself and others if you don't change. The normal human tendency is to try to force change through willpower. Instead, in Step 2, you realize that the only way to do it is to shift gears. You commit to a program that will help you slowly and patiently disentangle your life.

By the way, you now see why this program is described as both proactive (you are actively involved) and mindful (you cannot do it mindlessly, it requires your full attention).

Step 3

Moment by moment, I take a mindful pause to deal with my life calmly and effectively.

Original wording (AA):
Made a decision to turn our will and our lives over to the care of God as we understood Him.

Discussion of Step 3

Step 2 invited you to slow things down and find patience. It is tough to do so when the stakes are high. So, how do you do it?

Keep in mind the visual metaphor of disentangling a cord. It involves making space between the intertwined strands. How do you do this in real life, with intense situations that seem to require immediate action?

Two components

I suggest you think of any situation as having two components. There is the situation itself, and there is what it triggers in you. If you separate these two strands, you create more space for yourself.

I know the above paragraph is probably feeling very abstract. I want to give you a concrete example. Let's say you are playing baseball, getting ready to hit the ball with your bat as it is rapidly approaching. This is the first component, the situation itself.

Now, what is the second component? If you are calm as you see the ball approaching, you are best able to hit it at the right time and the right way. If you panic as you see it coming, you're not.

Even professional baseball players can go through bad streaks. They lose their ability to perform up to their usual standards. Same for golfers and tennis players. It's not just the situation itself, dealing with the ball. It is what the situation triggers at that time. Even highly talented and highly-trained professionals can crumble under pressure.

Dealing with pressure

So, it is essential to keep in mind that, as all human beings, you will at times be affected by pressure. You cannot fake being calm. Your priority is to find a way to restore calm.

To do this, you have to understand how deeply ingrained in us it is to be reactive. It is something that has been wired in us through the ages. Think about it in terms of evolutionary value. An animal or a primitive human who over-reacts might be wrong part of the time, but they will survive and have offspring. Those who under-react might be right some of the time, but they die and don't reproduce when they're wrong. In other words: evolution has favored those of our ancestors who tended to be very reactive. We inherited this trait from them.

Now, while this trait has been valuable evolutionarily, it is much more problematic in civilized life. It is inappropriate and even damaging in most of the circumstances of our life. For instance, when you play baseball, it doesn't work to see the ball as a threat that must be avoided.

Conversely, I'm going to give you an extreme example of what it's like to stay calm under pressure. Think about the action movies where the hero has to disarm a time bomb due to explode in the next few minutes. You and I would be so unnerved by the pressure that we would be unable to function. The heroes succeed because they manage to insulate themselves from the pressure, living in a bubble of calm as they focus on the problem.

When there is danger, our nervous system goes into fight-or-flight mode. It gives us a tremendous energy boost that makes it possible to run away or fight for dear life. All of our body resources are channeled into survival. As a consequence, there is little to no energy available for non-essential tasks, such as thinking. In a life-or-death situation, our ancestors needed to run away quickly or fight fiercely, not think. In the civilized world, complex problems cannot be resolved through fight-or-flight. It usually works better to fight smarter than to fight harder. And brute force isn't very good at disentangling a tangled cord.

The mindful pause

So, in the civilized world, we need to interrupt the reactive response that we naturally have and give ourselves a chance to see the situation accurately. It takes a mindful pause to do this.

The mindful pause of Step 3 is an acquired skill. We train ourselves to do it through repeated practice. The same way baseball players, tennis players, and golfers learn to slow down their movements mindfully.

You slow down what you're doing or even stop for a few moments. You shift your attention to what's happening in your body. Checking where you might feel some tension, for instance, in your neck or shoulders. Paying attention to your breathing, in your chest, in your belly. Nothing may come out of it. There's no pressure to perform. You're just making room for sensations, feelings, or ideas to come up if they do.

Turning over your will

What does this have to do with turning your will over to the care of God?

The above question refers to the wording of Step 3 in the Twelve Steps of A.A.

Literally speaking, the mindful pause has nothing to do with God. But, as in Step 2, we need to see things in context. The big picture in the Twelve Steps is to convince you to stop forcing change through willpower. Instead, you need to surrender to a more organic process. In the cultural frame of reference of the people who wrote the original Twelve Steps, the closest equivalent to that state of mind was surrender to God. Turning your will and your life over to God.

In the decades since then, much more understanding
of mindfulness has permeated our culture. These days,
it is possible to conceive of shifting from a willpower-
driven frame of mind to a more mindful state without
necessarily thinking of it in religious terms.

Step 4

I examine my life with honesty, searching for patterns in how I have been relating to people and situations.

Original wording (AA):
Made a searching and fearless moral inventory of ourselves.

Discussion of Step 4

At this stage, you are past the denial that you have a serious problem and need to address it. You have understood that you cannot force change. You have started to practice taking a mindful pause to see reality more clearly and calmly. With Step 4, you are now paying attention to your patterns of behavior.

To take an example, let's say you have been inappropriately rude to somebody. If you think of this as an isolated incident, all you need to do is apologize. Thinking in terms of patterns means taking into consideration different circumstances, different times, different people. You look at the way that several unrelated incidents may have some characteristics in common. Then, you can reflect on what it is that tends to activate you. For instance, what tends to make you angry or to overreact to the situation.

Of course, I'm only using anger as an example. You do this for any patterns that you notice. Bad patterns, such as anger, and good patterns as well. For instance, seeing that you are often generous.

Patterns

Thinking in terms of patterns is an entry point in understanding why you do what you do. Before you can effectively change anything, you have to understand why it happens. Because if you don't, then you don't have the tools to change it.

The original Twelve Steps called Step 4 a "fearless" moral inventory. The fearlessness lies in that you accept to face the reality of your fears. Not to be led by them, but to deal with them more effectively.

It isn't easy to do so. When we face uncomfortable truths, we tend to hunker down, feel defensive, come up with justifications. The only thing that makes this kind of honesty possible is removing the notion of judgment, that is, the potential for blame and shame. Step 4 is about looking at facts. Just facts, as opposed to adding overlays of judgment and blame onto them in such a way that the facts become obscured.

There is a big difference between being in Criminal Court and doing Step 4. In Criminal Court, the rule is for the indicted person to avoid punishment. In Step 4, your goal is to understand better what you're doing to be who you want to be.

Mindful understanding

We're talking about mindful understanding. This is different from trying to analyze and to force-feed some logic, some rationality into this. It's not that human behavior has no logic whatsoever. There is logic, but that is emotional logic. For instance, when you are scared, shadows on the ground will look threatening. When you are happy and safe, behaviors that otherwise might scare you will not be nearly as scary.

As I am introducing the notion of mindful observation, you probably see the link with Step 3. There, we were talking about finding clarity by taking a mindful pause. As of now, barely a step later, you have not yet perfected the art of the mindful pause and the art of finding serenity and patience in looking at yourself. But you're starting to be more aware of the difference between being in your default mode, between being in a kind of mindless state, and being at least a little more mindful. So now, in Step 4, you're making use of this growing ability to shift from mindless to a more mindful state. It helps you pay more attention to patterns in your life.

How to do it

To be mindful means, first and foremost, being curious and having the intention to stay as calm as can be, given the circumstances.

In practice, how do you do this?

You focus on a section of your life. For instance, when you were a very young child, when you started going to school, what it was like in high school.

Write about that period of your life the same way as if you were talking to a friend. Prompt yourself to write about friendships. About relationships. About work. About good moments and bad moments. You may start to see some patterns emerging.

If you are doing this with a friend or in a group, I suggest you take turns narrating a section of your life:

In any case, ask yourself what the possible common points between several of these stories might be. It takes curiosity and openness for you to notice patterns. It is OK not to see them right away. It's OK to spend quite a long time wondering what patterns there might be, if any.

Things will start coming up for you at some point or another, as you cultivate an attitude of openness and compassion.

In other words, the attitude you are cultivating is one of compassion. This builds up an inner sense of safety and trust which makes it more bearable to face reality.

Step 5

I explore these patterns and describe them to another person, noticing the healing power of compassionate listening.

Original wording (AA):
Admitted to God, to ourselves, and to another human being the exact nature of our wrongs.

Discussion of Step 5

Step 5 continues the process that started with Step 4. You are looking at behavior patterns, as opposed to just behaviors in isolation. In Step 4, you identified behavior patterns. Now, you are trying to understand them.

The vicious cycle

Before going any further, I want to address why it is essential to approach this process with self-compassion. That is, I want to talk about the pitfalls of self-criticism and the vicious cycle that ensues.

Here is how it goes. You do something that you would call a "wrong," and you criticize yourself for it. You feel ashamed of yourself. Through willpower, you manage not to do it for a while. And then, you slip.

You do it again. You feel ashamed. It's so unpleasant
that you end up indulging as a way to relieve the stress.
The vicious cycle goes on, alternating between
moments of willpower and moments of shame.
You have to step out of that cycle. For that, you need
to understand what is happening and take action earlier.

Understanding the emotional logic

Trying to understand your behavior patterns means
exploring why you do what you do. Is it just because
you're an evil, nasty person? Is it that you're so lazy that
you do things that hurt other people out of sheer
laziness? Or is there some method behind the madness?

There is usually some logic behind what you do. It is
emotional logic, not rational logic. You do your best to
understand it, as opposed to judging it and forcefully
eradicating it.

As you do, it is good to keep in mind the difference
between condoning and understanding. Condoning
would be trying to glorify the problematic patterns.
Understanding helps you change.

How do you proceed with exploring this?

Here, I'm going to describe sub-steps of Step 5 to
make the process clearer.

First, you're going to get a general sense of the
pattern. An impressionistic, fuzzy sense of what might
be emotionally behind what you do. Why, for instance,
you arrive late at your appointments. Or why you might
be angry at certain people. You go beyond the self-

blame, and you understand the reason behind it. And, probably, it's something like fear. So now you have a general sense of it.

Then you stay with it with curiosity. You try to work it a little deeper. You don't stop with that very vague sense of: "Oh, I'm doing it because it's fear," but you try to be a little bit more specific.

You stay with an example, a situation. You get a sense of what it felt like inside when you were in that situation, and you let the feelings come up. So it's not just an abstract concept, like "Oh, it's fear." Now, you recapture the experience. For instance, you experience tense shoulders, a constricted chest, or shallow breathing again. Or, maybe, that something in your stomach?

As you are reliving the physical sensations that you had been experiencing, you also visualize the situation. It is as if you were watching a video of it. Now, you have a felt sense of what the situation was like, from inside and outside. It is a felt sense, not an abstraction. And so, you now have more of a handle on what is happening.

Compassionate listening

Now, find another person, a friend, to talk to about what happened. Talking to another person helps means that you need to find words to communicate the experience more clearly than when you are on your own. Your friend asks you questions, which also helps you find ways to capture better what happened. As a result, you gain more understanding of your behavior pattern.

What you gain is not just better conceptual understanding. You experience the healing power of compassionate listening. You have a sense of spaciousness and acceptance.

If you are worried that compassion and acceptance will only reinforce problematic behavior patterns, keep in mind that accepting does not mean condoning. Accepting what is gives you the capacity to change.

What does this have to do with God?

The original Step 5 of A.A. talks about "admitting to God." Here again, it helps to think of this in context. For the people who wrote the Twelve Steps, the notion of redemption was intricately linked to the Christian religion. In the decades since they wrote the Twelve Steps, we have become more familiar with other ways to experience compassionate healing. In particular, we understand the healing power of compassionate listening. Ascribing it to God is optional.

Step 6

I understand how these patterns have been ways of coping with my fears.

Original wording (AA):

Were entirely ready to have God remove all these defects of character.

Discussion of Step 6

At first glance, it might seem like Step 6 is simply a restating of Step 5. We are talking here about seeing how your patterns have been ways of coping with your fears. How is that any different from understanding the emotional logic of your behavior patterns (Step 5)?

We are talking about subtle differences. Think about what the phrase "proceeding step by step" means. You're not rushing. You're paying attention to the details of what you are doing. So, here, you are going deeper into the emotional logic that you started to understand in Step 5.

Emotions

In Step 6, you are getting more in touch with the intensity of emotion involved in these patterns.

As you read this and think about your patterns, you may be surprised. You may not be aware of the emotional intensity in them.

Look at it this way. We are talking about behavior patterns that you seem to have no control over. You are doing things that you don't want to be doing. What is it that makes you do it?

Emotions are what moves us to action. Sometimes, we are conscious of them. Much of the time, we are not.

It is a feature of our brain and nervous system that very intense emotions drive us to react very rapidly. We are talking about split seconds, so fast that the information has not even had time to be processed by the more mindful brain circuits.

Why is that? Our remote ancestors needed to be reactive in the face of danger to survive. Those who were over-reactive survived better than those who dawdled too much. There was little reward for those that insisted on making sure there was danger before running away from the feral beast jumping at them.

Now, in civilized life, the nature of dangers has changed, even though our brain structures have not. The situations we face in our social interactions are usually more complex than the clarity in confronting a wild beast.

Reactivity

Reactivity had been a necessary shortcut to our ancestors in the wild. In the civilized world, this shortcut deprives us of using the mindful brain resources that would help us respond more adequately to the kind of situations we face.

And it all happens so fast that we are not even aware that it could have been possible to act differently.

So chances are you are not aware of the intensity of feeling behind your behavior patterns. You may not even be aware that the emotion led you to react so quickly that it didn't occur to you that you could have responded differently.

Being mindful involves slowing down the process to become aware of what happens so that it becomes possible to see the fork in the road. You cannot take it until you see it. And you cannot see it while you're under the grip of a powerful fear when your mind is reacting to what it perceives as a severe threat.

Fear and stress

Fear involves much more deeply rooted structures of the brain and the nervous system than thinking or acting through willpower. The more of a threat we perceive, the more we automatically revert to our most basic structures.

We cannot override the reactivity of fear through logic or willpower. When we experience a threat, our nervous system and brain bypass the more advanced, more mindful circuits. The more primitive, more reactive circuits take over for the emergency.

Overriding this natural process can only be done by calming the nervous system so that it can get enough time for the mindful brain to be engaged. Then we can process information and realize that things are not as dangerous as they first seemed to be. And so we can de-escalate the activation.

So, this step is about understanding overwhelm, that is, understanding stress.

Let's talk a bit about traumatic stress. Here's a well-known example of how people who suffer from traumatic stress can overreact to situations. A vet, back from the battlefield, hears a loud noise. To most onlookers, it may be startling because it's unexpected, but the shock of it dissolves quickly. Things are different for the traumatized vet. The noise triggers the sense of being in the battle zone, being shot at, or having a bomb explode nearby. To the vet, this is not just a thought or a metaphor. It is a virtual reality of the most convincing kind. The soldier, at this moment, is hijacked from present reality and re-lives the traumatic moment in all its intensity.

What it means to be triggered

Being triggered means re-living the traumatic situation of the past. You experience it as a very present reality. And you experience it in the way you did then, i.e., as somebody who does not have the resources to deal with it. You do not have access to the skills and knowledge that you may have developed since then.

So you are thoroughly disempowered. What the trigger brings back is not just a memory. When you're triggered, you are not in the present moment. You're experiencing what happened in the past as if it were happening now. And you only have the resources that you had then, not the skills you have acquired since. You are back in that overwhelming situation, just as overwhelmed as you once were.

So that's what you need to understand at this stage. It is why you do these things that make no sense. If it were just about logic, you would not do them. The problem is not an absence of logic. It's about safety versus danger.

What we're talking about here is undoing the effects of traumatic stress. Willpower alone is not going to be enough because fear is a much, much more powerful reaction.

Trauma is very powerful, so it may very well be that you cannot adequately handle it without help. You owe it to yourself to look for the help you need. One way is to find a peer group committed to providing a safe environment for all participants. Another is to seek professional counseling. Of course, the two approaches are not mutually exclusive; you can do both.

There is no shame in seeking help for something overwhelming. It is only the traumatized part of you that thinks there is shame in seeking help. And, if you listen to that traumatized part, you keep repeating the patterns that keep you traumatized.

Comparison with the traditional 12 Steps

In what way does this relate to the traditional wording of Step Six?

Step Six of AA talks about being "entirely ready to have God remove these defects." Don't take the wording literally. Think of it as describing a psychological process, not a miracle. That is: "It feels like I am ready for these defects to be removed."

To feel that way, you have to understand how these so-called defects are an attempt to cope with something that feels overwhelming. It is then possible for you to replace them with something else that fulfills the same function but works better and has fewer side effects.

Step 7

I learn to accept the sense of vulnerability that goes with life's pressures and uncertainties.

Original wording (AA):

Humbly asked God to remove our shortcomings.

Discussion of Step 7

The previous steps have led you to see problematic behavior patterns in a different light. You now get a sense of the emotional logic behind them. That is, they are ways of coping with things that would otherwise feel overwhelming.

What is it that is overwhelming?

Of course, the specifics vary. But, when you dig deeper, it comes down to the very opposite of feeling safe. A sense that you have no way of protecting yourself, that your very existence is threatened, that you will be crushed. "All resistance will be futile," as Darth Vader would say.

When you read this, you might say: "I can see how it might work for other people, but what I'm talking about is not that drastic."

So let's slow it down a little and explore. Go back to the fears that you identified in Step 6. Instead of just thinking of them as abstract words, go deeper into the physical sensation.

What does it feel like when you are imagining facing these situations that you fear? Let's pay attention to some of the markers that have to do with the experience of intense fear. There is, for instance, a sense of holding your breath physically. You might notice a tightness in your shoulders. You might feel that your shoulders coming up and your neck coming down as if bracing for a blow to come upon you. You might notice some weird sensations in your stomach. You might feel your eyes widen and how you are rigid, somewhat like a deer in the headlights.

What your body sensations tell you

Becoming aware of how your body is affected puts you in touch with the visceral quality of the fears.

Stay with these sensations, even for a moment, getting a glimpse of how intensely awful it feels. The difficulty of it gives you more understanding of why you're not able to stay with them in everyday life. And that gives you more of a sense of why the coping mechanism exists and why it continues.

The coping mechanism is essentially a way to avoid staying in what is literally an unbearable experience. Getting in touch with the physicality of the experience and how much it blocks you helps you understand why words and logic are not adequate at such moments.

Your mind and body automatically do whatever it takes to stop that unbearable pain. And that's where the coping mechanism comes in.

We are talking about a mechanism of avoidance, but not in a way that would justify self-blaming. When you pay attention to the intensity of the experience, you understand better how you have no other choice at that moment. It's not about willpower.

If not willpower, what is the way to deal with it?

Essentially, the idea is to become more tolerant of that unbearable feeling progressively. Gradually become more able to tolerate how awful it feels. Realize that you can feel that bad and still survive it. As you do this, little by little, you develop the ability to live through the pain. You become able to have more choice in what you do, despite the pain, instead of automatically defaulting to the coping mechanism.

So the principle is straightforward: There is unbearable pain. You learn to stay with it, little by little. As you do, you start to notice that you have options. Of course, what is very simple in theory is excruciatingly hard in practice. Here again, we have to recognize the importance of avoiding the very damaging cycle of self-blame. When you say to yourself: "Look, it's so easy. How come I can't do it? If I can't do it, it's terrible, and so on," this is not helpful at all.

Safety

In contrast, what is very important is to focus on a sense of safety. To foster a sense of nurturing, a sense of encouragement. So, whenever you see yourself reverting to a sense of pressure and blame, remember that what you're dealing with is related to overwhelming fear.

You are experiencing a sense that you're going to be crushed, that you're defenseless. What you need more than anything else is a sense of safety, a sense of protection, a sense of support to be better able to face this enormous threat.

There is absolutely no point in trying to minimize the threat by saying: "Oh, objectively, it's no big deal. So if I realize how it's no big deal, I should be able to deal with it easily." These are should, not reality. The point is you perceive something that feels like a genuine threat to your very existence. There is no reasoning with that kind of fear. You have to address it at the gut level. What it takes is reinforcing your sense of safety. Once you are safe, you have options. In the middle of fear and pressure, you don't.

And so, what is of foremost importance is developing ways to reinforce a sense of safety. I will come back to it a little later.

If you cannot feel body sensations

I want first to address something that you might be wondering about. When I described the physical sensations of fear in your body, you might be among the many people who don't experience that. You feel numb. Or you might not even experience yourself as emotionless. You might say: "I don't experience anything abnormal. I'm just here. What's that?" If that is the case, you might then think that everything else I've been talking about after that does not apply to you. Well, I want to kind of put this into a different framework. When the intensity of fear is extreme, a standard human coping mechanism is to dissociate from the experience. So I suggest that you do not take it at face value that your lack of sensations means that you are not having a sense of overwhelming pressure. If you are indeed somebody who has problems doing things that you don't want to do, chances are the coping concept applies to you.

I suggest you feel curious about what there might be under that sense of: "Oh, nothing's happening" or in that numbness.

Take it for granted that there might be something, even if, at this moment, you cannot feel it. Be curious about it. You're going to make it an essential part of your life to understand it better. Gently, without undue pressure, without forcing yourself to find it right away or in the next few days or even in the next few weeks.

A physical sense of vulnerability

Having said this, I can come back to what you do to create safety to stay longer with that physical sense of vulnerability.

One way to do it is to develop your physical sensations as a resource. For instance, build your ability to notice what happens when you breathe a little deeper. Or when you do some gentle stretches, not necessarily full-fledged yoga movements, just moving in a mindful way. Or when you pay attention to the flow of blood and air moving through your body. Notice the sense of feeling more grounded in the way you're sitting or standing up. Notice how these things help you come to a more grounded emotional state.

Another resource is talking to people, friends, acquaintances, and peers engaged in a similar exploration process. People with whom you can gently share your experience as part of this exploration and who can share with you their own so that there is a sense of trust. You share a common goal. You want to progressively open up to things that might feel way too much for you to experience or deal with on your own. Because, with pressure and overwhelm, you might be cut off from even the experience of it. So, dealing with it in a gentle, supportive group is something that's going to be helpful.

Of course, it never hurts to seek professional help. As we've talked about before, this is something that's in the continuum of traumatic stress. It doesn't hurt to find all the help you can get.

I want to emphasize that we're talking about exploring, not changing behavior patterns. The Twelve Steps process proceeds step-by-step. Actual changes are going to come later. Right now, you're not pushing. You merely have the goal to progressively, slowly expand your ability to tolerate the intensity of sensations that accompany those problematic situations.

What about asking God?

Step 7 of A.A. is "asked God to remove these shortcomings." Again, it helps to see the reference to God in context.

For one thing, it is a signal that changing profoundly ingrained behavior patterns is a slow process. It is not: "I see the pattern, and I immediately wipe it away." There are several steps in the process. One of them, Step 7, is just "asking God," which might feel redundant with Step 6, which was about "being entirely ready." Talk about an excruciatingly slow!

It is slow because it is akin to disentangling a tangled cord: you cannot do it if you're not patient and careful.

So, what do you do with this time? While the original Twelve Steps refer to asking God, the Proactive Twelve Steps describe a psychological change process. You cannot get rid of a coping mechanism until you are able to deal with the vulnerability that the coping mechanism was covering up for. Hence, this step is about accepting vulnerability.

Step 8

I explore alternative behaviors and rehearse them in safe settings.

Original wording (AA):
Made a list of all the people we had harmed, and became willing to make amends to them all.

Discussion of Step 8

Here we are very much in the thick of the step-by-step approach to changing dysfunctional behavior patterns. By now, you have much more understanding of why it's not a "Just Do It" attitude. We are talking about behaviors that have risen to cope with something overwhelming.

"Overwhelming" is something you feel at a gut level. To make changes that are effective and sustainable, you have to go slowly. It makes it possible to address the problem that caused the avoidance and coping behavior.

So, in this step, you are not yet making changes in real life. You are exploring and practicing possible changes in the privacy of your mind. That is, not with the intensity that is involved in interacting with others.

Baby steps are not just for babies

You might think that this is too much of a baby step. Well, it helps if you put it in perspective. Just look, for instance, at boxers. Practice in boxing is not limited to fighting. It involves using a punching ball. You also practice improving your form.

In martial arts, judo, karate, Aiki-Do, people spend a lot of time learning the movements slowly and deliberately. They practice the form in addition to doing practice fights. And all of this practice is not just for beginners. Even highly advanced martial artists do that.

There is something similar in golf. You visualize the movement. You practice it when you are not playing golf, i.e., when there is no pressure. Practice helps you learn better.

A practical example

Let's take a simple example. Let's say that the behavior pattern you want to change happens at work when people interrupt what you're doing to ask you to do something for them.

As we have seen in Step 3, there are two components to every situation you're in. There is the situation itself, and there is what it triggers in you. Taking a pause allows you to pay attention to the two components.

You take a pause and reflect. The situation is the interruption, other people asking for something. The other component is how you respond. Your knee-jerk reaction is to reflexively say yes. Now, this has a cost to you: you end up being overextended. It also has consequences for other people. As you take on more than you can handle, you don't deliver on some of your promises. You get impatient and resentful, which doesn't make it pleasant to work with you.

In Steps 5, 6, and 7, you have paid attention to the emotional logic of what you are doing. You have a sense of the level of pressure and fear that it brings up for you. So you understand why your automatic answers are what they are. And now, in Step 8, you are brainstorming some ways in which you can respond to people differently.

To do this, you look back at past situations. What happened today? Last week? What other moments do you remember? In Step 8, you look at them to see how you could have done something differently.

Do you have a minute?

Let's take an example, an interaction with a colleague at work, let's call him Tom. He popped into your office, or your cubicle, and said: "Do you have a minute?" Reflexively, you said yes. But you did not have a minute. You were in the middle of something.

When you listened to Tom explain whatever he wanted to tell you, you were in a state of inner frenzy, all tied up in knots because you could not hear him. You were still thinking about what you needed to do for

yourself. You were between two chairs, neither in one
nor in the other.

In the brainstorming part, you rewind the imaginary
video to the moment when Tom said: "Do you have a
minute?" And you then imagine yourself raising your
head slowly, facing him, and saying: "No, actually,
Tom, sorry, I don't have a minute right now. Maybe we
could talk about it later this afternoon. Would 3 o'clock
work for you?"

You are not reflexively saying yes. You are not saying
no either. You're finding a way to be respectful of your
needs as well as the needs of the other person.

Now, this will seem obvious to people who don't
have a problem with managing interactions. But if you
have this problem, it may feel hard even without the
pressure of the actual encounter with Tom. It brings up
the sense that you don't have the right to say no. You
believe that you should be available whenever people
want you to be.

The practice consists of challenging this belief.
However hard it is to do it in a practice session, it will
be less hard than to do it when you're not in the heat of
the action.

A clarifying comment

I want to emphasize that you are not looking for
magic words. The goal here is to confront your
dysfunctional beliefs. I wanted to give you an example
of dealing with it in a rehearsal mode.

As you practice, pay attention to the feelings that go with saying something as simple as: "No, Tom, actually, sorry, I don't have time right now" and notice how it feels inside, what your breathing is, what your tensions are, how stressed your voice might be.

Embracing the tension

Chances are, even in a rehearsal situation, if something is emotionally difficult for you, you're going to feel stress. The idea is not to hide it. It's not to pretend you're not rehearsing to play a role. If you notice tension, that's great. Embrace it. The stress tells you that there is more emotional work to be done. It means that you're not ready for prime time, which is OK. It means that you still have more exploring to do, and that's OK.

The point here is you're not trying to fake it, to pretend it's easy for you. You are exploring patterns in situations where you have difficulties, so it is not easy to change. You are doing this exploration for yourself, not to impress other people. Figuring out where the problem is will help you find a way to address what is difficult. Again, the idea is not to look to others as if you were relaxed about it. It is to figure out what makes you tense and stressed out, so you can deal with that adequately. And that's why you're going, slowly, step-by-step.

What about the people you have harmed?

The original Step 8 of A.A. advises you to make a list of all the people you have harmed and become willing to make amends to them all. In the Proactive Twelve Steps, Step 8 is more comprehensive. You don't just prepare to apologize. You figure out a way to avoid hurting people in the future. Of course, you will apologize to people you have hurt. Your intention to apologize is much more meaningful now that you have thought about how not to hurt them.

Step 9

*I apply these new mindful behaviors in my
everyday life. I sincerely apologize to people I have
hurt, except when counterproductive.*

Original wording (AA):

*Made direct amends to such people wherever possible, except
when to do so would injure them or others.*

Discussion of Step 9

So far, we have been emphasizing a sense of going
slowly, step-by-step, to better deal with what is
blocking you from doing what you want to do. But
eventually, there comes the point where the rubber
meets the road. You put into practice what you have
been preparing for.

The key here is to stay mindful

It's not an either-or proposition. It's not either you
change your behavior, or you are mindful. It's both. If
you only focus on your conduct, it may happen in a
blur, as you are forcing yourself to do what you believe
you should be doing. You will likely be tense, not quite
emotionally present as you're doing it. This kind of
change will not be lasting, and it's not going to be

satisfying. You're adding stress and pressure to your life. In some way or another, it's going contribute to your level of general and happiness and lead you to act out. So, it's no good.

Applying things in real life does not mean forcing yourself to look from the outside as if you're doing it. It means being present, mindful, grounded in doing it.

Recalibrating your expectations

Since we're talking about changes that have to do with coping mechanisms, these changes will be difficult. The changes will not be smooth, and you're not going to feel comfortable about that.

So if you expect that it should be smooth, you're going to be disappointed. I want to recalibrate your expectations so that you're realistic. You're going to be noticing all kinds of turbulence inside. And that is good.

Conversely, if you expect that it all flows naturally and effortlessly, you're going to be disappointed. You might disconnect from your feelings to not notice how stressful it is to apply these new behaviors in real life.

I want to emphasize that the behaviors we are talking about are coping mechanisms because situations that trigger them are very stressful. As a result, you bypass the difficulty and go to a default mode. The bypass is related to the intensity of the stress that is generated by the situation.

It hardly matters how much you have rehearsed alternative behaviors. When it comes time to implement them in real life, you're back into the stress of the situation. And so it would be astonishing if it went smoothly. I would like you to be ready for that.

Remember that it's going to be emotionally challenging to make these changes. You're going to have a hard time trying to be emotionally present and mindful as you try to behave differently. So you need to engage your curiosity toward noticing how not present you are, how stressed you are, how difficult it feels. The turmoil is not strange. It is the lack of discomfort that would be strange.

A practical example

To make it a little more practical, let's go back to the example we used in Step 8. We talked about somebody who has difficulty saying "no," not just to new projects, but even saying "no" to people coming in and interrupting to talk about something. And so let's say you're that person.

In Step 8, you identified some ways to behave differently. For instance, say Tom comes into your office, asks if you have a minute, and you say: "Oh, sorry, Tom, I can't do it right now, but what about this afternoon at 3?"

When you hear me say that, it feels OK. There's no stress or pressure in my voice. But when Tom comes into your office, this is not the case. You are feeling jittery, feeling nervous, having difficulty looking at Tom in the eye. Your voice is strained. You might feel some sense of shame about it or, at least, feeling very uncomfortable. And that's OK.

Anticipating this kind of turmoil and stress is going to help you calm down the inner critic. The inner voice that would say: "Oh, you messed up. You'll never be going to be able to do that." Anticipating the turmoil as typical and predictable will help you find a response to the inner critic: "No, wait a minute. This kind of turmoil is normal."

It is quite possible that you feel that your delivery sounded odd, that Tom might be looking at you in a way that implies:" What's a matter with you?" If so, you could respond to Tom: "Hey, I know I might sound a bit incoherent here, but that's a reflection of how busy I am right now. So that's why I can't give you my full attention now."

If you think about it, you see how this awkward moment might help you make your point.

All of this is to give you an idea that the difficulties are not crazy. They are manageable. You can manage them, and you can go beyond the turmoil instead of adding further stress and pressure to a situation that already has plenty of that.

Comparison with the traditional 12 Steps

Now, I want to address how the Proactive Step 9 corresponds to and differs from the traditional wording of Step 9.

The similarity in both approaches, for Steps 4, 5, 6, 7, 8 and 9, is that we are taking a step-by-step approach to deal with the difficulties instead of sidestepping them. But there is also a significant difference.

In the traditional Steps, the focus is on misbehaving. The concept that you're doing something wrong, you're hurting others, and you have to eventually find a way to apologize to them, which happens in Step 9.

With the Proactive 12 Steps, we're not limiting the nature of the change to doing something morally reprehensible and making amends for it. We're talking about paying attention to behavior patterns that are not what you want to be doing. Then, the focus is on understanding them to find better alternatives for your own sake and others.

Obviously, to the extent that you hurt other people, you're going to apologize to them. That is part of your learning to interact with people differently. But it's not as narrow as in the traditional 12 steps. It's a much broader context.

Now, you mean it

An apology that is just an apology without changing behavior is nice, but not that great. It is much better to change how you act so that the apology corresponds to a genuine change. From now on, you are going to behave differently. Not because you're going to force yourself to, but because you're a changed person, and you can now act differently, naturally. And so, as you apologize, it is not an empty apology, but one that is grounded in the possibility of acting differently.

Step 10

I keep paying attention to the causes and effects of my actions. I act accordingly.

Original wording (AA):

Continued to take personal inventory and when we were wrong promptly admitted it.

Discussion of Step 10

When you read that Step 10 is about continuing to pay attention to the causes and effects of your actions, you might feel that it's a bit restrictive. Aren't you already past that?

After going through steps 4 through 9, you could legitimately feel that you have turned a page. Indeed, you are much more aware of what it is that makes you do what you do. You have identified patterns. You have understood what is behind them. You have deeply understood how to change these patterns and apply these changes in real life.

Despite all of these achievements, Step 10 implies that you will misbehave if you stop paying attention. It's good not to take things for granted, but there is a danger in being hypervigilant.

Living in fear of yourself

If you live in fear of your nature, you feel cramped. You fear that, at any time, you might do something terrible. So you have to always be on your guard.

Not only is it unpleasant to live with that sense of having to be constantly vigilant, but it's also counterproductive. It adds to the pressure you are already feeling. You probably don't need more of it in your life. Adding pressure keeps you in a hopeless loop, a vicious cycle: You keep pushing, pushing, pushing to improve, to be the best that you can be. As a result of pushing so hard, you are cracking under too much pressure. This cycle feeds itself.

What we are talking about in the Proactive 12 Steps is something very different. Instead of fostering a sense of distrust in your abilities, you acknowledge your accomplishments and build on them. You see how going through steps 4 through 9 has been helping you understand yourself more. You see that this has been helping you more of the person you want to be.

There is a sense of pleasure and liberation in being more aware of who you are and feeling able to change what you don't like. There is a lot of satisfaction in being able to do this moment by moment. When you feel this way, the process of Step 10 is very pleasurable.

It is the opposite of feeling rigid control, living in constant fear that you will be doing something terrible. Instead, you are enjoying being conscious of your life. You are enjoying the mastery of being able to be who you want to be moment by moment.

Mindfulness as liberation

Ultimately, being mindful does not mean adding to your burdens. It is satisfying, as opposed to something that is imposed on you to cramp your style. To use a practical example, let's say that you intend to be mindful when you eat. You would like to notice and enjoy your food. Suppose you turn this into an internal critic that is constantly criticizing the way you eat. In that case, you turn this into a nightmarish experience.

It's much better to see it as an opportunity. You say to yourself: "I might be more conscious of how I eat and of how I enjoy my food." When you notice that you're eating without any sense of satisfaction, you don't criticize yourself and put pressure on yourself; you don't force yourself to find joy. You just notice: "Gee, isn't it strange how I don't find satisfaction in eating?"

Noticing gives you an occasion for pausing and wondering. You might then ask yourself: "Was there a moment when I enjoyed even a small part of this experience?"

It may very well be that all you want is to have your belly full; you do not take any pleasure in the moment-by-moment experience of eating. The point is not to force yourself to experience something you are not experiencing. It is to start a dialogue with yourself. You begin to understand better what happens. Little by little, you give yourself a chance to find something that works for you. It's not a pre-imposed thing. It's not a mold that you have to fit into, or else.

Engaging your curiosity

The same goes for paying attention to the causes and effects of your actions. It is possible that, at this point, the process of mindful awareness described in Steps 4 through 9 does not give you much of a sense of pleasure. You might see it as cramping your style. You might be longing for the possibility of not having to pay any attention. If this is the case, it's good to notice it. And then, it's not a question of then forcing yourself to pay attention or trying to avoid it altogether. Instead, it is an opportunity to be curious about what makes you uncomfortable with this process. Very gently. You're not trying to shoehorn in a new habit. You're trying to understand better what it is that makes it uncomfortable for you. Little by little, as you know it, you have a higher possibility to change it.

The idea is that you consider that it might be possible for you to be happy and satisfied when you're more mindful of your life. You don't force yourself to be aware. But you explore how the way you pay attention makes you unhappy, or cramped, or impatient, or somewhat flooded. As you stay with it, new opportunities open up for you. You come to understand that the goal is not to cut off parts of you for you to become something that corresponds to some abstract idea of good. You have a growing sense that this is a process of liberation and expansion.

Step 11

I make space in my life for mindful reflection. A sense of meaning and purpose naturally arises from that.

Original wording (AA):
Sought through prayer and meditation to improve our conscious contact with God as we understood Him, praying only for knowledge of His will for us and the power to carry that out.

Discussion of Step 11

Step 11 is a way to expand into the experience gained throughout the whole process. Here, you are building upon the lesson of Step 10. This time, you are not just paying attention to the causes and effects of your actions. You are mindful in all aspects of your life.

Mindful living

What you have gained throughout this process is not just a better understanding of yourself and the ability to change behaviors, however important that is. Over time, you have started to learn new habits, new ways of living. The new ways of living are not just behaviors. They have to do with the attitude you have toward living life, moment by moment, mindfully experiencing life.

The change is not just in how you act. It is in how you approach life. Mindfulness is not a means to an end, however practical and beneficial it is to accomplish your goals. Being mindful is an end in itself.

Now, of course, the goal of being mindful all the time could be incredibly overwhelming. Besides, it is unrealistic. We are not talking about some perfectionistic notion. What we are talking about is a practical sense of mindfulness. It involves the practice of pausing, moment by moment. We talked about the mindful pause way back, in Step 3.

Now we are circling back to that. We are going back and saying: "OK, you have paid a lot of attention to all kinds of things about your life. You have made changes, but let's go back and pay attention to that skill that you have developed during that time."

Taking a mindful pause

You may not have consciously developed the practice of taking a mindful pause. However, you have been practicing it just by doing what you did. You have been paying attention to your behaviors. And you have been noticing what it feels like when you are avoiding what feels painful or challenging.

By paying attention to what it's like to change a behavior, you have developed your ability to pay attention to your inner sense of self. So, don't worry, as you approach Step Eleven, even if you feel: "Oh no, I never practiced the pause very much, if at all." You likely did. You would not be here if you hadn't. So this step is first an invitation to notice the many ways in which this kind of mindful pause has become more ingrained in you.

Mindfulness is not just something that happens when you stay cross-legged, recite a mantra or count your breath. There are many mindfulness meditation techniques. But mindfulness is not limited to these techniques. There are different ways to be mindful. It helps if you remember that mindfulness essentially means being more able to pay attention to what you're doing and be present with it. For instance, thoughtfulness is very much part of mindfulness.

With a mindful pause, you give yourself a chance to notice the default mode. You see what you do without thinking. You give yourself a chance to notice that there might be alternatives. It does necessarily mean that the other options are better. You may not even have to act differently. It's just that you are giving yourself a chance to notice. It's a way of slowing down. It's a way of feeling that you have more options. In doing that, there is a calming effect. There is a grounding effect. There is a sense of opening and expansion that happens. Don't you want more of this in your life?

Under pressure and fear, there is a sense of having no options. Being under pressure feels like you are caught in a vise, and the walls are squeezing you. The opposite of that experience is the ability to extend both arms and to push back against the walls. Then, you feel that the walls are moving back, and you're gaining more space.

A sense of peace and possibility

Wouldn't you want to have more of that in your life instead of pressure and fear? Wouldn't you want to have a sense of space and calm and peace and possibility?

Taking a mindful pause gives you a chance to find more space. Step 11 is about giving that to yourself, moment by moment. It describes facing reality mindfully, moment by moment. The notion of "facing reality" might not feel very appealing if you're accustomed to hearing about "facing reality" in the context of criticism. That is, you have been repeatedly accused of not facing reality. From that perspective, "facing reality" is a punishment. It is like rubbing your nose into something that smells bad, that you've done. So, if that's what "facing reality" is, you have every reason to avoid it.

But think about what you've learned about yourself through this Twelve Steps process. You have found a way to contemplate unpleasant things about yourself in a way that was more gentle and kind. It is more geared to understanding than to harshly criticizing yourself. In so doing, you have found that you were able to change the things you didn't like about yourself in a way that felt more pleasant, more satisfying, more rewarding.

You have been building a sense of confidence that is replacing the old tapes.

The old database of experience said that facing reality is a punishment, and you're safe when you avoid reality. Your new database of experience shows that you can face reality mindfully, moment by moment, and it helps you grow. It helps you feel more satisfied and happier. You now have more reason to want that in your everyday life. Not because it's some abstract idea of what a good person should do, but because you have a growing sense of how much you ultimately like it. This is what it's like to experience a felt sense of meaning and purpose.

What about conscious contact with God?

The original Twelve Steps of A.A. refer to prayer and conscious contact with God. As in previous occasions where God was mentioned, it is helpful to think about the underlying experience. What Step 11 describes is the experience of feeling a sense of meaning and purpose, i.e., something that is similar to what a religious person might experience as being "in the hand of God." The words are different, but the experiences have a lot in common.

A similar comment can be made about the notions of prayer and mindful reflection. The cultural context is different, but the underlying experience is similar, a deep connection to something very meaningful.

Step 12

My life reflects a growing sense of respect and compassion for myself and others. I share this process with others who are struggling.

Original wording (AA):

Having had a spiritual awakening as a result of these Steps, we tried to carry this message to alcoholics, and to practice these principles in all our affairs.

Discussion of Step 12

What does it mean to have compassion for yourself? Essentially, this is what you've been doing throughout these steps, instead of harshly judging yourself.

What you have learned

Instead of forcing yourself to do something against the sense of fear or hurt you experience, you have been trying to understand what made you do what you did. You have learned that sustainable changes are changes that you are happy with, as opposed to changes that you force on yourself through some abstract idea of what you should be doing.

Throughout this process, you have learned to be aware of, respect, and understand different parts of yourself that may conflict. You have been finding ways to get unstuck based on a better understanding of the forces in conflict.

As you stay with this process, you realize that it is not just you; it is human nature. So that adventure, that journey you had in understanding yourself better, is not just about understanding the specifics of the situation. It is also about understanding the way it affects all of us human beings. You now see your experiences as part of the human condition. Your struggle is simply the form that it takes for you. Every human being experiences some form of suffering or another.

Kinship with others

Through your experience of suffering, you may be drawn especially to those people whose kind of struggle is closest to yours. For instance, it makes sense for alcoholics to gather together; this fosters a sense of kinship. They feel they understand each other better because they've been going through some very similar challenges, which unites them. The same thing goes for other Twelve Steps programs for various forms of addiction.

The Proactive 12 Steps are not just for people who are dealing with addiction. They are for all human beings dealing with the pressures, fears, and difficulties of the human condition. In theory, you could connect with any other human being based on joint suffering from the human condition. In practice, it is easier to get close to people who are more like you.

As you go through this program with kindred spirits, you get to see that the kind of suffering you have does not set you apart from the rest of humanity. It is the specific way in which you are experiencing the human condition. And so your heart opens up to better understanding other people in the world, as you feel a kinship with them.

Feeling a kinship with others does not necessarily mean that you understand the specifics of what happens to them. It might be dangerous to think that you fully understand anybody. If you felt that way, you might get more closed instead of wanting to hear about their experiences because you'd feel like you already know. It is dangerous to assume that you automatically understand how other people function.

Through your suffering, you come to appreciate the value of becoming closer to people by being compassionate with their plight. And you become more aware of the possibility of finding some common ground if you dig deep enough.

A deeper understanding

Through these steps, you come to understand your experience in a very different way from the way you did when you started. You're freer from polarized thinking that sees the world in terms of good and evil. You have a more complex, more nuanced understanding of the fears and pressure that led you to adopt coping behaviors. You have become more comfortable staying with the excruciating difficulty of feeling vulnerable.

And you also know that you have not entirely resolved these things. You are far from perfect, and that's okay. The more you know about yourself, the more you are aware of how much is still unknown. You know that you have gained some degree of comfort in some situations but still feel stress in others. You have reached a superhuman level of understanding that makes you impervious to all the challenges, fears, and pressures of life. On the contrary, you know how vulnerable you are. You know a lot about your limitations, but you can live with that or certainly can live with it more than you used to. You don't have to be perfect to be okay.

And so it is that a greater understanding of your vulnerabilities makes it possible to connect more with other people. This kind of connection is very different from what preaching would be.

Preaching involves a sense that you are in contact with a transcendent truth that you want to force-feed others. You are sure that, if only people listened to you, their life would be better.

A gentler attitude

The kind of truth that you have come into touch with is much softer. These are not absolute truths about: "Do this!" or "If you believe this, your life will be better!" Your insights are very nuanced. They are more about the inevitability of vulnerability and the fleeting quality of moment-by-moment experience. They are also about the possibility of finding a sense of having more space, of expanding, having more satisfaction in life, and staying with that.

These are not things that you were able to get by forcing yourself. You got to that by progressively expanding your comfort zone by dealing with vulnerability. This attitude is what you want to bring in connecting with others.

Conversely, you are not doing this outreach just out of the goodness of your heart. It is not that you are such a fantastic person, helping others who are in dire need of your words of wisdom to get better. You are seeking connection because you have experienced how connecting with others who are willing to face their vulnerabilities helps you. Now, you know that being helpful to others helps you as well.

Part 2:
A mindful & proactive roadmap

I have long had a deep interest in the processes of change and growth, which led me to become a therapist and life coach. What interested me in the Steps is that they describe a process of transformation that does not require a therapist or a coach. It seemed to work for quite many people, but I wanted to better understand what made it work.

I started re-writing the Twelve Steps to better understand the process they describe. I decided to "translate" the wording of the Steps into language that felt clearer to me.

I'm not just talking about language that would make each step more straightforward. I am talking about articulating the Steps in such a way as to clarify the process of change that they describe: what it is and how it works.

The following provides some thoughts on this process as I see it.

Stop self-defeating behaviors now

In Step 1 you have the stark realization that you have been in denial. You have a problem that you can't ignore, and what you've been doing about it has essentially been making things worse.

You might then expect that the following steps would be very sharply worded injunctions to stop your self-defeating behaviors. You might also expect specific instructions on how to do it.

Instead, only Step 1 refers to self-destructive behaviors (e.g., alcohol). In these Proactive Twelve Steps, while Step 2 refers to dysfunctional behaviors, the only purpose of this reference is to explain how the healing process works.

Why is that? It is not that it has suddenly become OK again to go into denial and keep behaving the way you were. It is assumed, at this point, that you realize the absurdity of clinging to these behaviors.

Stop now

You need to stop. There is no doubt about that. But this is not a reason to say it eleven more times. Step 1 very clearly states that what you've been doing has serious consequences. Whenever you forget this, please go back to Step 1.

We will talk more about how willpower is not enough to achieve lasting change. Chances are, you may relapse into your old patterns. This is not a reason to postpone making needed changes.

Use your willpower to stop now. Take it for granted that there will be ups and downs. This is part of the process. This is why you are not relying only on willpower, but following a more comprehensive program.

Name the specific problem(s)

Often, there is more than just one problem behavior. For instance, a workaholic may also be prone to anger, or abuse alcohol, or be codependent in relationships, or all of the above.

It's not enough for you to say: I tend to do things that are self-defeating. The opposite of denial is facing the problem squarely. It would be best if you named the specific behavior(s). For instance: My codependency in relationships is self-defeating. Or: My overeating is self-defeating. Or: My anger is self-defeating.

Try it. If you're not comfortable with it, if it makes you squirm to name the specific problem(s), you're probably still in denial. It means it is still so painful for you to face the problem that you avoid facing it. You don't need to force it, but it's good for you to be aware of it.

"I" vs. "We"

If you are familiar with the Twelve Steps, you will immediately notice that the Proactive Twelve Steps are written from "I" instead of "we."

It was a deliberate choice, but not an easy one. I will talk more about the reasons for this choice after acknowledging the strong arguments in favor of the "we" of the original Twelve Steps.

The "we" perspective conveys a powerful message: You are not alone. You are part of a group that has overcome what is too daunting for any individual to successfully confront independently.

From the first time you read the Steps, you can feel that you are part of a successful group. The "we" also reinforces the notion that success is not something that one achieves through sheer willpower, fighting alone against the way the world works. Success involves following a path that others have already taken.

So, why not maintain the "we" for the Proactive Twelve Steps?

Essentially, the "I" statements convey the sense that this is a personal journey of self-discovery and self-development. You confront complex issues, make choices, and learn from experience. Self-confidence literally refers to the growing confidence you have in yourself.

It does not mean you are alone. You seek support from others and acknowledge it. But you have a sense of being actively involved in the process of change. You are proactive and mindful. Your attitude reflects a growing sense of responsibility for yourself: "This is important to me, and I will do what it takes."

This is also why the Proactive Twelve Steps are written in the present tense instead of the past tense. They focus on the moment-by-moment struggle to find serenity, courage, and wisdom as you deal with the challenges of life. Being mindful means living in the present moment.

Much of the process described in this book involves learning from experience the difference between trying to force change through willpower and being proactive in a mindful way. Suffice it to say, at this point, that the "I" of the Proactive Twelve Steps is not a lonely "I" trying to force change through self-deprivation. It is an observing "I" that is deeply attuned to inner processes and interactions with other people.

In this sense, it is an "I" that has learned to accept the realities of the world. But this acceptance does not mark the death of the self. It is just the death of a lonely, desperate, powerless "I" and the birth of a much larger, more flexible, more effective, and much happier "I."

Serenity, courage & wisdom

Through trial and error, I develop the serenity to accept what I cannot change, the courage to change what I can, and the wisdom to know the difference.

Original wording (Reinhold Niebuhr):

God, grant me the serenity to accept the things I cannot change, Courage to change the things I can, and the wisdom to know the difference.

Discussion

The "serenity prayer" describes the process and the desired outcome of the Twelve Steps.

A prayer?

This wording is an adaptation of what is known as the Serenity Prayer. Does this mean that you have to pray for it to work?

Despite all the "Let go and let God" talk, the Twelve Steps are not advocating that people do nothing but wait for the grace of God. Keep in mind that most of the steps are about ways to change your attitude and behavior.

The "prayer" part emphasizes how important the qualities of serenity, courage, and wisdom are. So crucial that religious people would be asking for God's help in achieving them.

If you're not religious, skip the "prayer" part. Keep in mind the valuable advice: The process of change involves learning by trial and error. As you go through it, you develop your ability to be serene, courageous, and wise. In turn, this helps grow your ability to make complex changes.

Serenity

Change does not happen by forcing yourself to be somebody you're not. And it certainly does not occur by blaming yourself for the things you're not doing. Progress comes from deciding to understand what it is that is happening. You don't fight reality; you accept it.

If you cannot change it, you're not going to keep banging your head against a wall. But finding serenity does not mean that you are abandoning any hope of change. You are merely figuring out where you have a grip, some possibility of changing, and where you don't. You are orienting your efforts toward where they may bear fruit.

Courage

Courage does not mean pushing yourself to do things that won't work. It does not mean jumping out of a tenth-floor window because you dare yourself to do that. If you keep doing things that don't work, it's not courage. It is more like insanity.

Courage lies in confronting your vulnerabilities, accepting them, and staying with them. Doing this is very different from bluster. It is much softer but also much more intense, much more difficult. You're not avoiding feeling the difficulty, but you're learning to stay with it.

This is the courage to remain emotionally present as you face your vulnerabilities, to learn from the discomfort, to grow from it. Not to close your eyes and ears and nose and force yourself to do something so unpleasant that you can only do it by avoiding being emotionally present.

Wisdom

Wisdom comes from experience, that is, trial and error. Often, you don't know in advance what you can change and what you can't. It's not that easy to figure it out ahead of time.

As you go through these Twelve Steps, you are giving yourself the chance to learn from experience. So, the "wisdom to know the difference" is the wisdom that you gain from experience.

To gain wisdom, it takes the courage to confront challenging situations. It also takes the serenity to realize that there is no value in keeping banging your head against a wall. Time and again, you are learning to redirect your energy toward where it may be more productive.

Serenity, courage, and wisdom are three facets of the process of lasting change. Giving them distinct names helps you pinpoint what you're doing. This enables you to own the process for the rest of your life.

A broader context

There are plenty of times when people do things they don't want to do. Addiction is an extreme example of this. But addiction is only part of a broad spectrum that includes compulsive behavior, habits that are hard to shake, Freudian slips, etc.

Instead of looking at these occurrences from a moralistic perspective, it is more productive to approach them in a spirit of mindful inquiry. That is, to ask two related questions: "What is it about this situation that I cannot change?" and "What is it about this situation that I can change?"

Asking these questions helps us let go of the all-or-nothing paradigm ("I can change it all?" vs. "I cannot change it at all"). It helps you pay attention to the nitty-gritty of what you can, or cannot, do.

From this perspective, the Serenity prayer is not so much a prayer as a proactive call to mindful action. It is not about reaching an ideal state of serenity, courage, or wisdom. It is about operationalizing courage and serenity, i.e., asking the questions that help you make sense of life and gain wisdom.

The shifts of Steps 1 to 3

The process described by the original Steps seemed to me to have many of the trappings of religion. It's not just that they explicitly referred to "turning our will and our lives over to the care of God." It's also that the Steps talked about becoming a good person in terms of rights and wrongs and defects of character.

The tone felt similar to the religious language of sin and redemption. To oversimplify, the process they described looked like the following: (1) You realize you're a sinner. (2) You repent. (3) You are touched by the Grace of God, and your life changes.

What makes it work?

Does this mean that the journey of the Twelve Steps is essentially a religious process? That is: Are the key ingredients faith in God and conversion to a set of rules inspired by this faith in God? Or is there something else at work? If so, what causes the healing? And how can this be expressed in terms that are not obscured by moralistic, religious, or mystical connotations?

Let's look at the Steps with these questions in mind, starting with Step 1. There's something a bit puzzling about this step. "Admitted we were powerless" is so incredibly obvious that you'd think it may not be necessary to say it. And yet, that is precisely where the breakthrough is. You get to understand that the logic of your coping mechanisms is to prevent you from seeing the obvious. Essentially, the first step in this process is to realize that you're not going to go anywhere until you face reality.

From this perspective, the language flows easily. Step 1 is a simple realization: "I face reality. I am not able to control what I do, and this has serious consequences."

Let's continue to look into the other steps from this perspective, which means looking squarely into things, not letting any obfuscation hide reality. Wow! We bang right into a wall as early as Step 2. The original wording of Step 2 brings us right into a mystical leap of faith: "Came to believe that a power greater than ourselves could restore us to sanity."

OK. Let's not get bogged down by the literal meaning of that phrase. What is it about? Maybe it's a way to say that there is some leap of faith involved in this process? But does this mean it has to be religious faith? Blind faith into some mystical powers that dwarf us and defy understanding?

What is faith?

Faith is too powerful a part of the human spirit to let religious people have a monopoly on it. Just think of the phrase: "Faith moves mountains." We're not just talking about religious faith here. We're talking about the power of the human spirit. That is, the capacity to focus on what matters, even if the chances of success are minimal. The ability to not feel defeated by the low odds of success and rise to the occasion. The "faith that moves mountains" is our human ability to find the motivation and energy that increase our chances to accomplish the impossible.

Let's go back to our dialogue with Step 2. We ask of it: Don't just ask me to believe in mysterious forces. Tell me more specifically: What is the leap of faith involved in Step 2? Faith in what?

Before directly addressing the question, let's take a little detour, and reflect on the Twelve Steps as a whole. The Steps were originally written by alcoholics. Yet, they are not a guide to dealing with alcoholism per se. Other than telling you to face the issue squarely (in Step 1), the original Steps do not give any specifics about alcoholism. Instead, they describe a journey of profound personal transformation.

In other words, the central insight of the Twelve Steps is that the effective and sustainable way to deal with alcoholism is to counterbalance the pull to addiction by building a stronger sense of self. Now, a phrase like "stronger sense of self" may sound abstract. Concretely, this means living a more satisfying life built on a foundation of integrity.

Integrity

Note that the word "integrity" may be confusing if you hear it to mean something like "righteous" or "self-righteous." It is different if you keep in mind the spirit of Step 1, facing things as they are. You see that this is not about behaving in a way that others would say you are "doing the right thing." It is about doing what feels right for you. Truly right, deeply satisfying, not just right in the sense of following your impulse of the moment for instant gratification. It is about allowing yourself to discover that you can eventually get more satisfaction out of life by resisting your compulsions. This ultimately leads you to lead a life that is more deeply satisfying for you.

Time has shown that this process works. It is powerful enough to counterbalance the pull of addiction, not necessarily for everybody who has tried it, but for many people.

However, this is far from obvious when you're in the thick of it. If you're dealing with self-damaging habits, it's not evident at all that making the kinds of profound changes described in the Twelve Steps will help you. It may even seem crazy, like a luxury you can't afford at the time. The changes feel daunting. So why would you undertake them at all? It takes a leap of faith to do so.

Faith, yes, but not necessarily faith in God. You have to have faith that the solution lies in changing the structure of your life. As long as you keep behaving in a short-term, reactive way, you stay in the vicious cycle of addiction. You need to take a proactive stance, change the pattern. You need to realize that you are more likely to revert to old patterns if you don't have a solid sense of self and a solid life to anchor you.

A shift in perspective

The original Twelve Steps describe in moralistic terms (e.g., defects of character) the side effects of living in a reactive mode driven by fear, pressure, and

shame. You experience life in a fog, with a sense of fear
and confusion. The journey is how you get from that
place to fear and confusion, to a sense of safety and
integrity. You get to shift from being scared, defensive
and reactive, to feeling more grounded and able to be
proactive.

Now, Step 2 becomes clearer. It is about seeing the
big picture. Hence: "I understand that I cannot force
change through willpower. I need to disentangle my life
patiently."

This leads us naturally to Step 3, breaking the
vicious cycle of fear and pressure on a moment-by-
moment basis. "Moment by moment, I take a mindful
pause to deal with my life calmly and effectively."

And so it goes. Each of the Proactive Twelve Steps
is based on looking at the original Steps from the
perspective of facing reality and talking about it in a
down-to-earth manner.

Over time, as you go through these Proactive Steps,
you get more and more of a felt sense of the big picture.
That is: under stress, you experience a sense of intense,
visceral certainty that you're lost unless you stick to your
old coping mechanisms. In actuality, these coping
mechanisms are harmful to you. But these are just
meaningless words to you at the moment when you
experience intense stress. You need something to "keep
the faith" moment by moment to avoid relapsing into
self-defeating behaviors.

Over time, the Steps help you get progressively more
able to overcome these challenging moments, much like

exercising makes you physically stronger. They guide you on a healing journey to gradually develop a healthier sense of self. As your life becomes more and more satisfying, the old coping mechanisms lose their compulsive attraction.

The notion of ecosystem

Starting with Step 2, you have acquired a new perspective. To break an unbreakable habit, you don't focus doggedly on the habit itself. You change your life so that this bad habit becomes obsolete. Your new life supports habits that are good for you. In other words, you focus on the person as opposed to the habit. You put your efforts into changing the ecosystem. You build an ecosystem that will support the life you want.

Let's talk more about the notion of ecosystem now that you are starting to examine the patterns in your life.

How are patterns formed?

A paradox of the human condition is that our tremendous ability to learn can be a great asset and a significant liability. The downside of our ability to form and reinforce habits is how solidly ingrained bad habits, including self-defeating habits, can become.

We generally don't acquire bad habits with the intention of doing something harmful. Usually, these habits start as a coping mechanism, i.e., a way to deal with an otherwise unmanageable situation. They get reinforced through a dual action that feels like a carrot and a stick. The "stick" is the pressure and fear that drive us to react. So, we go with what we know without examining alternatives. The "carrot" is the relief and the dopamine reward that follows the coping reaction.

The intensity of the relief and reward, on the one hand, and the pain and fear, on the other hand, make a mockery of our efforts to eradicate bad habits through willpower alone.

The word "eradicate "is a good one, especially if you remember that this word stems from the Latin word for "roots." If you think of a habit as a tree, you can see that it is connected to the ground through a network of roots. These roots not only provide nutrients for the tree; they also anchor it solidly in the soil. The older a tree is, the more difficult it is to uproot it.

Thinking in terms of ecosystem

An ecosystem means that various things work together as a whole to support each other. For instance, think about how bees and flowers work together. It takes the flowers to feed the bees, but it takes the bees to pollinate the flowers.

Thinking in terms of the ecosystem means thinking that there is interconnection, all of the parts work together. Think about the phrase "a habit that is deeply rooted." It evokes a network of firmly planted roots that makes a tree that much harder to uproot.

To sustainably change a habit, we need to understand what this habit is a solution to, however imperfect it may be. We need to find a better solution. We need to find a new ecosystem that gives us an environment that is at least as good as the old ecosystem.

Keep in mind the image of roots as you think about the habits you want to uproot. Or another image, a stone wall, built by laying stone upon stone upon stone. It's impossible to remove a stone at the bottom because it is held in place by the weight of the others.

These metaphors complement the metaphor I used for Step 2, the disentangling of a tangled cord. They illustrate why it is so daunting to change an ingrained habit. What makes it hard to change is that it's interconnected with a lot of other things. It's part and parcel of life as a whole. So, essentially, to change a well-ingrained habit, you have to change your life as a whole.

The old ecosystem keeps reinforcing the bad habits. You need to build a new ecosystem to support new habits. This is what you do with the Twelve Steps.

An example

If you want to change a habit, it is good to avoid the people, places, and things that trigger that behavior.

Emily, who wants to stop drinking, says: "I go to the bar every day after work, and I drink with my friends." If she only focuses on her failure to stop drinking through willpower, she overlooks other considerations that might be relevant. For instance: Other possible ways of relaxing. The possibility of finding other friends. Or, is her work a source of more stress than she can handle?

Asking these questions is not a way to find excuses for what she does. The point is to give herself a solid foundation to understand why she does what she does and change it effectively.

Little by little, she will be making changes in her life. She might develop friendships that are around something other than drinking. She might find different ways to relax. She might conclude that the job is not right for her and change jobs.

In other words, she will be changing the building blocks of her life. She will develop an ecosystem that makes it possible for her to have a satisfying life without drinking.

In a nutshell

Why do the 12 steps talk so much about life change and so little about habits that need to change? If habits are difficult to eradicate, think of them as intertwined with the fabric of your life. Keep in mind that your life as a whole reinforces them. So, you need to change your life if you want to succeed in changing these habits.

Codependency

Initially, the term "codependency" was used within the context of the Twelve Steps. It described a pattern where family members and friends "enabled" the dysfunctional behavior of the alcoholic because of their enmeshment.

The word "codependency" is now widely used. It mainly describes relational dynamics where people have difficulty being themselves while being in the relationship. Mostly, they confuse interdependency and codependency.

Codependence vs. Interdependence

Interdependency is a normal, healthy, essential part of being human. It is not so for codependency. In codependent relationships, the partners have difficulty finding a balance between being themselves and being in the relationship. Instead of finding the right balance, codependent people are at the extreme. Either they are subsumed into the relationship or assert their independence aggressively and destructively.

Often, codependent people feel that they "should" be independent. It leads to black-and-white, all-or-nothing thinking. Either you are independent to the point of being unrelated, or you are codependent!

But you cannot be both in a relationship and independent. The challenge is to be interdependent:

recognizing that you need your partner and your partner needs you, but both also need to be individuals.

Being part of the couple vs. being a separate person

In any relationship, people are mutually dependent (that's the very definition of a relationship). Therefore, people in a relationship will inevitably experience tension between the pull to see yourself as part of the couple and see yourself as a separate person.

Think of it as a slider on an electronic appliance:
– One end of the slider corresponds to the position where the only thing that counts is the couple;
– The slider's other end corresponds to the situation where the only thing that counts is being a separate person.

Neither of these extreme positions is workable:
– If the only thing that counts is being a couple, you are stifled as a person.
– If the only thing that counts is being separate, then there is not much common ground for being a couple.

So, the slider needs to be someplace in between. This place will vary moment by moment, situation by situation.

This place is what codependent people have trouble with: They have difficulty with the flexibility of moment-by-moment adjustment. They are more likely to be in an all-or-nothing mode – – all accommodating to the other or seeing any demands of their partner's as pure selfishness.

Conflicts (or lack thereof)

I am pointing out that there is an inherent conflict to being in a relationship. The art of relationships is to manage conflicts, not avoid them as if they were shameful "proof" that you are a dysfunctional couple. In fact, what is dysfunctional in a couple is to avoid conflicts. Growth lies in learning how to manage conflicts effectively.

In a healthy relationship, this can be dealt with openly. As a result, both partners can progressively feel more secure in the relationship. They can be more intimate at the same time as they grow as individuals.

With codependency, these issues are more challenging to deal with. Often, they are swept under the rug. Or they're dealt with in an atmosphere poisoned by accusations of selfishness. Or one partner finds a way to intimidate the other. As a result, there is a growing backlog of resentment between the spouses.

A symptom of codependency is the extent to which desires and demands are not fully expressed, mostly hinted at. Usually, this is because there is a fear of conflict. If you ask for what you want, you fear that your partner will be hurt or angry, which will be unpleasant for you. On the other hand, you can't bear to stay silent. So you say something, but in such a covert way that your partner won't get it. This behavior is a perfect recipe for feeling unheard, frustrated, and resentful.

All too often, what happens is that each partner feels they have an implicit agreement with the other — but the other is not aware of this unspoken agreement at all. Hence the sense, on both parts, that there is something fishy going on, that the other is in bad faith. The antidote to this is to build a safe environment, i.e., to make room for each partner to fully express their needs and wants.

Related to this is the sense of "you owe me." You do something for your partner that you don't want to do. You convince yourself to do it by telling yourself that, this way, your partner will owe you a favor. But you don't say this to your partner at the time you do what your partner wants. You only mention it much later, when you are trying to cash in the favor, and your partner acts surprised and angry, and then you feel betrayed!

Feeling constrained

Another symptom of codependency is a sense of feeling "hemmed in," constrained in the relationship. It is in sharp contrast to feeling spontaneous and free. It feels like you cannot do or say what you want because it will either hurt or anger your partner.

Now, of course, expressing what you need and want does not mean that your partner is obligated to give that to you. Part of what makes the relationship safe is that there is no sense of coercion. If your partner expresses what they want, this does not mean that you have to give it to them. The point is not that you have to sacrifice your own needs without any hesitation. The point is that you need to learn to negotiate and to tolerate the inevitable frustrations that are part of the negotiating process.

Until such a time as you can make room for these frustrations, there will be a sense of despair and anger every time there is a conflict. You will tend to see your partner as a source of frustration, as the source of your unhappiness. And vice versa. As a result, there will be a lot of blame and finger-pointing.

Blame is a significant characteristic of codependency: "It's your fault!". This not very different from what happens when kids bicker: "But, mom, he started it!". Bickering kids would very much like to have a grown-up validate their feelings by punishing the other kid. Ideally, grown-ups can go beyond these feelings to resolve their differences between themselves. Resorting to blaming makes it harder to understand each other and find common ground. The blame game seems to turn into an ever-escalating cycle, where it becomes increasingly harder to stop and acknowledge each other.

For codependency to heal, partners must agree to create safety in the relationship. You do so by consciously avoiding blaming, shaming, dismissing each other, or stonewalling as a passive-aggressive response to actual or perceived attacks.

Lack of intimacy

There is a paradox with codependency. On the one hand, you are very connected. On the other hand, there is a genuine difficulty with real intimacy. It is difficult for the two of you to drop your guard to feel relaxed, comfortable, and vulnerable (in a good way) within the safety of the relationship. So you avoid intimacy. You or your partner have too much to do at work or with the kids. You are too tired to make time for special moments. Here, I am not just referring to physical intimacy but emotional closeness as well.

What next?

What do you do if you see many of the toxic characteristics of the codependent profile in your relationship?

Life would be easier if your partner would "see the light" and be willing to change. Unfortunately, this is something you have very little power over, if any at all.

A typical codependent reaction is to believe that nothing can be done unless both partners in the relationship work at it. Of course, it's much better if you both work at it. But, if your partner doesn't want to, you can still do something very productive, both for yourself and for the relationship. The power you have is over what you can do, from your end, to deal with codependency. So you do your part, regardless of what your partner is doing.

A creative dialogue with your inner critic

There's a ferocious voice that keeps pointing out
your shortcomings. It shatters your self-esteem with a
harsh putdown when something goes wrong. And it's
tough to run away from this voice: it is the voice of your
hostile inner critic. You can't silence it. Let's examine
how you can have a creative dialogue with it.

Understanding who the inner critic is

When you hear the inner critic, especially when it is
loud, it is good to remember that it is compensation for
feeling vulnerable. At that moment, there's a part of
you that can feel powerful by bullying another part of
you. It is helpful to remember that this fierce inner
criticism is a symptom of feeling vulnerable.

Look for what it is that makes you feel vulnerable.
Be gentle with it. Sometimes, facing the issue makes it
a little less scary. Even when it doesn't, it's good to
remember that, in staying with it, you're "building
muscle" for the long run.

Let's take the case of self-criticism with self-
defeating habits. It goes for smoking, eating certain
foods, overeating, drinking, getting out of bed late, you
name it. You keep hearing yourself say: Why can't I
stick to doing (fill in the blank) when I know it's good
for me and I need to do it?

It should be easy

The implicit assumption is that it should be easy. If only you had a little more discipline, a little more willpower. So you criticize yourself: "All it takes is a little discipline, and I don't even have that!".

Sounds familiar? Well, this is the voice of the internal critic. When you hear this voice, you feel shame: "This critical voice is right, isn't it? I'm a horrible person for not doing this simple thing that's good for me".

What gives this voice tremendous power is that there is some truth to what it says. It would be easier to silence that negative voice if it was always wrong. But the problem is not that the voice is incorrect or only partially correct. This inner criticism makes it much more difficult for you to do what you need to do.

Now, you might be wondering: "Are you saying that I shouldn't do the things that are right for me?" That's not what I mean. What I mean is that the critical voice is not helping. It is not finding solutions. I am saying that the critical voice distracts you from the task at hand.

Do nothing

What, then, am I suggesting? Essentially, to do nothing. Just for a while. Just listen to your internal dialogue. This is how you'll see what this is all about.

This kind of situation often reflects a conflict: Different voices inside you are fighting for different things. There's one — the one you're aware of, the one that appears to be the voice of reason, asking you to do what's right for you. And there's probably also another voice, muted but very powerful, that holds you back.

What I'm suggesting is that you test this hypothesis. Take time to listen to your internal voices for a few days. It might be a week; it might be a bit more. During this time, give yourself permission not to do the "disciplined" thing that's good for you.

Does this mean you're giving up?

Now, you say: "That's terrible. That's giving up. How will I ever make any progress if I stop trying?"

Just remember — you're not doing what's good for you right now. You're just trying, or, actually, just saying that you're trying. There's not much of a loss if you give yourself permission to not doing it for a few days — you're just accepting reality.

I know it's not necessarily easy. That's part of the struggle. You do it, and you observe how it feels to do it. You notice the thoughts and feelings it brings up. You remind yourself it's an experiment, one that is limited to a few days. This experiment is about helping you know yourself better.

Let's say you're paying attention to the struggle you have about getting up in the morning. It's morning, and you're in bed. You know you have to get up. And you won't. You're noticing this, and this probably brings you back to the internal dialogue you usually have in the morning about that.

The Angel & the Devil

So, when you notice that, stop. Try something else. Try to be creative about it. Make up a dialogue between the Angel and the Devil.

In cartoons, you know how they sometimes have these two characters battling for influence over the hero — the Angel and the Devil. The Devil will say something like: "Come on, just one more drink. One for the road." And the Angel will say, "You've had enough already," or words to that effect.

Imagine you have a Devil and an Angel floating somewhere around you, trying to influence you. Let them speak, listen to them.

You may then notice a third voice — one that says: "Come on, this is ridiculous. Stop this silly exercise, it's not leading anywhere". When that voice comes, notice it, acknowledge it... but ignore it, and go on. What you're doing is worthwhile. You are exploring. You're listening to what happens where you have trouble. You're getting valuable information.

Listen to the dialogue

You listen for a while — it could be a couple of minutes; it could be hours. It depends on you. It depends on the day. Write down what's going on. You can write it literally — if you do your "listening" while sitting down with pen and paper. Or you can write down the highlights after the fact. Add a sentence or two as a way to summarize your reactions.

Now, what do you do on a morning where you have
no difficulty getting up? Just write a couple of sentences
about how you feel, about what makes it easy for you to
get up this morning.

Shifting the goal

What's happening is you're shifting the goal. Instead
of forcing yourself to do something you have difficulty
doing, you now focus on better understanding what is
happening inside. As a result, you can figure out what
works for you.

Lasting self-confidence stems from a sense of
knowing who you really are. This includes facing the
inner critic, keeping it at bay, and hearing the negative
self-talk without believing that it is the whole truth
about you.

Once you have asked yourself the difficult questions,
you think positively because you know who you are,
what you can do, and what you honestly can't.

How dysfunctional behaviors make sense

We usually think about dysfunctional behaviors as something that does not make sense. It helps to see them as having a logic of their own, something that has to do with our capacity to learn from experience. In this context, dysfunctional behaviors can be described as coping mechanisms.

First among the coping mechanisms are the early coping strategies that we adopt unconsciously to deal with our environment as children. They stay with us, pretty much unconsciously, for the rest of our life. Typically, we are not aware of having any coping strategies. However, we see them, sometimes glaringly, in others: the character types in the human comedy, the miser, the greedy person, the braggart, the coward.

Thinking in terms of early coping strategies helps us step away from the blaming tone of "character defects." It also helps us put the difficulties people encounter in changing habits or dealing with addictions within a broader context.

Adaptation

Human beings have a great capacity to adapt. In that, we are not unique: All life forms are good at adapting. We are exceptionally good at it.

Think of adapting as a coping strategy. For instance, when you see a tree growing sideways instead of straight, you understand it as how the tree "coped" with being in the shade by going in the direction of the light.

Our coping strategies are more complex because we are more complex organisms than a tree. But they are based on the same principle. For instance, our attachment patterns reflect how we responded to our original family environment.

It is hard for us to be aware of our basic coping strategies because they are deeply ingrained. We are so accustomed to them that we cannot see them. Even when we become aware of them, it is extremely tough to change them. Trying to do that through willpower alone is often a recipe for failure. Why? For the reason that we call it a coping strategy, i.e., something that has to do with allowing us to survive.

Survival

Evolution has honed in us mechanisms that reinforce habits that help us survive and inhibit habits that could endanger us. So, our coping mechanisms are constantly reinforced, but trying to change them triggers powerful inhibiting mechanisms. To the amygdala area of our brain, trying to change a coping mechanism is as threatening as trying to put your finger into the fire. You're going to get burned if you do it, so don't do it!!!

Trying to change a coping mechanism triggers intense fears about survival.

Fear is a fundamental, profoundly ingrained driver of behavior. Willpower is largely ineffective against it in the long run. If you overlook the survival function of coping mechanisms, you will fail to change them. In contrast, taking a mindful and proactive approach means that you are prepared for the backlash that inevitably follows attempts to change.

The process of Steps 4 to 10

There is a significant difference between the
Proactive Twelve Steps and the original Twelve Steps
in describing the central process of behavior change of
Steps 4 through 10.

The original Twelve Steps reflect the moral and
religious outlook of their authors. Behavior is described
in moral terms: "moral inventory," "defects of
character," your "wrongs." The "return to sanity" feels
similar to redemption through the grace of God.

In contrast, the Proactive Twelve Steps do not use
the language of sin and redemption any more than they
see healing as happening through the grace of God.
Instead of talking about wrongs and character defects,
they focus on behavior patterns. That is, what you do as
opposed to your being flawed as a person.

The scope of the Proactive Twelve Steps is different
as well. We are not just talking about what is
traditionally considered addictive behavior, things like
drinking or gambling.

The scope includes any behavior that you do as a
knee-jerk reaction. For instance, looking at your cell
phone compulsively or being impatient with people.
Things you find yourself doing time and again as if you
didn't have the power of choice.

The focus is internal

We are not talking in moral terms, i.e., good and evil, as defined from an outside perspective. We are talking about doing yourself a disservice by repeatedly not doing what would be right for you.

The approach of the Proactive Twelve Steps is to help you find the power of choice, moment by moment. Yes, this result happens to coincide with what some people would call a moral improvement. But your focus as you work on the Proactive Twelve Steps is not on moral improvement. It is on being present, moment by moment, so that you can see alternatives to your knee-jerk reactions.

The context of the Proactive Twelve Steps is not judgmental because criticism is not effective in changing coping mechanisms resulting from fear, pressure, stress, and trauma. Instead, the focus is on understanding the emotional logic that leads you to do what you do.

Traumatic stress

Here is a classic example of why it is essential to put behaviors in the context of what created them. Take a veteran back to civilian life, who hears a noise, feels attacked, and wants to fire back at enemies. We now know enough not to condemn the traumatized soldier for being traumatized. We understand that the trauma needs to be healed.

Trauma is not a character defect. It is a normal consequence of dealing with a level of pressure that is so overwhelming that a person does not have the resources to handle it when it happens. Adding additional pressure in the form of moral judgment does not solve the trauma. Far from it, it makes it worse. It adds insult to injury. It compounds the problem.

Admittedly, the language of sin and redemption may be motivating to some people. But it can be very harmful to many people, as it adds more pressure to what already is a high-pressure situation. What can ensue then is a vicious cycle of guilt, shame, and more stress.

You feel ashamed of yourself. You try to force yourself to act differently through willpower. You succeed for a while. And then the pressure is such that you break down. You get temporary relief as you break down. But then, the shame comes back, and you use a lot of willpower to try and ward off what you are trying to ward off. And the vicious cycle goes on and on.

The vicious cycle can only end when you recognize that adding more pressure will not solve the situation. It only makes things worse. Of course, this does not mean giving up on making changes. It just means making them in a way that is more realistic and, actually, more effective.

What it means to live in the moment

The phrase 'live in the moment' feels a bit intimidating to many people, as if it was referring to some vaguely mystical state. It is very concrete. Imagine you're playing tennis, and you have been doing badly with your serves. Or, for that matter, imagine you're playing golf, or baseball, and having a bad streak. Chances are you would be getting more and more tense, more and more flustered.

If it were possible to live in the moment totally, you would be able to treat each serve as if it was the only one. Your mind would not be preoccupied with the increasing background noise about the earlier moves, and all the internal pressure that is mounting as a result.

In practice, of course, it is tough to do so. Even people who are trained to perform under pressure have a hard time with this. Witness the temper tantrums of professional tennis players.

Our nervous system is highly reactive.

We are wired to respond to danger. As soon as we perceive what might be a danger, we automatically get into fight-or-flight mode. Which means, we're flooded with a lot of energy. We also have decreased blood flow to the brain (i.e., we are less smart), and we have reduced peripheral vision. All of this is perfect to single-mindedly do what it takes to survive, e.g., strike an opponent or run away. But not that great for playing golf or tennis, or for most other post-paleo activities.

By the way, that fight-or-flight reactivity is very much 'in the moment.' In fact, what could be more 'in the moment' than the ability to do what it takes to survive?

So, the problem is not so much: 'how to be in the moment'. It is: 'how to be in the appropriate moment.' There are times when it is appropriate to have hair-trigger reactivity (maybe not so many in our modern lives). And moments when it is much more suited to tame that reactivity to have better access to our other resources.

The somewhat mystical goal of 'living in the moment' can be restated in a more down-to-earth way. The goal is to proactively manage our reactivity so that we can respond to situations as they are, unencumbered by our baggage and projections.

In a nutshell:

- There are plenty of times in our modern life (vs. paleo times) when reactivity is not appropriate.

- To override reactivity, thoughts, and willpower alone are not going to be enough. Reactivity is hard-wired in us, as it has been useful for survival through millions of years of evolution. What it takes is training the nervous system.

- We do this the same way we improve our athletic or musical or other skills - through practice.

From reactive to proactive: Mindfully dealing with vulnerability

Reactivity has tremendous survival value. It is what happens in fight-or-flight, i.e., when the sympathetic nervous system is activated. This automatic reaction has developed in all animals to help us survive in case of clear and present danger.

Much more recent evolutionarily are the functions of the human brain that allow for a broader assessment of the situation beyond the knee-jerk reaction to danger. Neural circuits in the frontal cortex will enable us to determine that it is not actually that threatening even though something feels like a significant threat. This process allows us to downgrade the alert from DEFCON 1 to something more appropriate.

Mindfulness is the human ability to engage the more evolved neural circuits. This process is a sort of due diligence to improve the quality of the information that we get through our reactive brain circuits. I am not talking about ignoring our more primitive reactions; far from that. I am talking about building upon these primitive reactions. Instead of reacting impulsively, we use this reactive impulse to start a more sophisticated process that helps us respond more effectively to a given situation.

Given how some people think of mindfulness as an esoteric practice, it is essential to state that what I am describing here is a natural human ability. We function more effectively by discriminating between what is a manageable threat and what is not.

Now, how do we do this? Of course, it helps to have the intention to make the shift. It helps, but it isn't nearly enough. We are talking about overriding a potent mechanism, one that has been reinforced by millions of years of evolution. This mechanism enables us to mobilize enormous amounts of energy in the service of survival when we face what we perceive as a significant threat. The bigger the perceived risk, the more overwhelming the task will feel. Pushing against the fear will only increase the sense of pressure and danger and make it even more difficult to override the reactive impulses.

Reactivity means fear

When you're reactive, you may not perceive your reactivity as fear. For instance, you may feel confused. Or feel stuck. Or you may be very angry, even angry to the point of being scary to other people, in a way that doesn't sound like you're afraid. So let's not call that fear. Let's call it "intense emotion, related to a sense of threat." The point is, it is the sheer intensity of the emotion that makes it hard to override.

How does one deal with this? I'm going to take a simple example in which managing the "threat" is relatively easy. Let's talk about what happens when you start wearing contact lenses and how you get accustomed to inserting them into your eyes.

You put the lens on the tip of a finger, and you start moving the index finger toward your eye.

What do you notice?

You automatically close your eyelids as the finger is approaching. You are doing this even though you're moving your index slowly. And, of course, you know that this is not an attack on your eye.

So you need to pull down the lower eyelid with one finger of the hand that has the lens, and pull up the upper eyelid with the other hand, to keep the eye open.

You notice that the eye tends to close despite the fingers holding the eyelids open. This reaction is happening even though the movement of your finger toward your eye is slow and controlled.

Fortunately, this operation becomes more natural over time, as your mind learns from experience that there is no risk.

Learning to overcome reactivity

This learning is possible because many factors are helping you override the reactive impulse to the perceived attack. For one thing, you know that millions of other people have made this gesture and that the medical profession is behind it. But also, the finger that moves toward your eye is your own so that you can modulate the movement. In other words, there is less of a threat because you have control over the action. As you feel safer, there is less of a need for a protective reaction.

Conversely, you wouldn't be able to relax enough to keep your eye open if somebody else's finger was coming at you fast. It would be impossible to override the perception that this is an attack.

To override reactivity, you need to feel safer

You can't feel safer through logic alone. Logic helps, of course, as it does with contact lenses: It helps to know that eye doctors think of this as a safe procedure. But it is not enough. What is necessary is the experience of actually feeling safe. This way, the powerful protection circuits of the brain can relax their grip and make change possible. Remember that these protective circuits are those we share with other animals. They are more primitive than our cortical circuits. They are not good at the subtleties of complex thought. To overcome reactivity, you need to experience a visceral sense of safety. Why? The function of reactivity is to protect you. It becomes unnecessary if you have another way to feel safe and protected.

We are talking about a visceral sense of safety and an intuitive understanding of the intense emotions that have a grip on you. We cannot achieve this kind of intuitive understanding when trying to get at it by only using words and logical discourse. The brain circuits involved in these emotions do not have the sophistication to process complex concepts or logic. So we need to pay attention to moment-by-moment physical experience. We need to keep coming back to that instead of staying solely at the level of "talking about" what might be happening.

Focus on bodily experience

There is a transformative effect in paying attention to bodily experience in the context of developing our ability to self-regulate. You need to pay attention to what is happening in your body instead of your thoughts. It helps you shift focus to what is here and now. It enables you to be in the moment in a way that you cannot be if you try to "be in the moment."

Focusing on bodily experience redirects your attention from abstract concepts to the present moment.

This shift in focus is a form of mindfulness practice, a skillful means to enhance our natural ability for mindfulness and proactivity. Over time, there is a progressive training effect, building up your resilience, similar to the way you develop your body's strength and resistance through physical training.

Part 3:

A perspective informed by neuroscience

We have a tremendous capacity to adapt and change. This is very clear when we look at the big picture, our history as a species. We have been able to adapt to a range of very diverse life conditions, geographically, economically societally, and radically different from the environment in which we originally evolved.

Our capacity to change is also evident at the micro-level, i.e., when we observe the structure of our brain. We keep forming new neural networks in response to our experiences, not just in childhood but also throughout life.

So, the issue is not that it is difficult for us to adapt and learn. The issue is: Given how good we are at adapting, why is it that, in some cases, we find change so difficult to make?

Asking the question this way hints at the answer. What makes it challenging to change is the fear that change would put us in great danger. We are not resisting change. We are reacting to danger.

So, it helps to understand how our organism manages threats. This part of the book is based on the Polyvagal Theory developed by a distinguished neuroscientist, Stephen Porges.

Later in the book, Appendix 3 features a conversation with Dr. Porges.

The three circuits of the autonomous nervous system

In the environment in which we evolved to become Homo Sapiens, threats were a normal part of life. The goal was to respond to them appropriately. We will review how our organism deals with threats.

The Polyvagal Theory describes our autonomic nervous system as consisting of three circuits. They represent three stages of development throughout evolution into more and more complex animals and human beings. Keep in mind in reading the following that each circuit functions as a way of managing interaction.

The Shutdown circuit is the most primitive. It is akin to an on/off switch. When faced with an unmanageable threat, the organism essentially shuts down, conserving energy. The Fight-Flight circuit provides added functionality. It allows for significant energy boosts to deal with threats. For instance, the gazelle gets super-charged to run away from the lion. The Mindful Engagement circuit is the most recent and most sophisticated. It evolved to mediate social engagement, a crucial functionality for the social animal that we are. It allows us to deal with the nuances and subtle complexities of life.

The Polyvagal Theory observes that these circuits are activated in a very specific order, the reverse order in which they came to be.

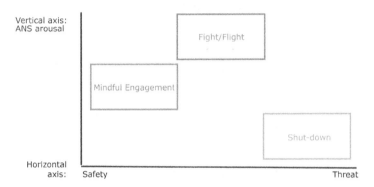

The Autonomic Nervous System (ANS) / Polyvagal Theory

We first attempt to respond to threat through the Mindful Engagement circuit, our most sophisticated circuit. Now, if this system is so good, why aren't we using it all the time? Think of it in terms of trade-offs. A sophisticated system requires a lot of energy. This means that there is not much energy left for dealing with safety. The Mindful Engagement circuit works beautifully when the threat level is relatively low. It is not appropriate with more intense threats.

When the threat level intensifies, it becomes essential to deal with the danger rather than get mired in subtleties. Our nervous system then shifts to the Fight-Flight circuit. This system gives us a burst of energy, which allows us to face danger head-on. In the environment that we evolved in, this energy had an immediate use. Our ancestors would use it to either fight or run away.

In some situations, Fight-Flight is not sufficient to deal effectively with the danger. In the presence of an overwhelming threat, our nervous system then shifts to the third circuit. This is the Shutdown circuit. When all resistance is futile, we collapse, or we automatically shut down and disengage. The benefit is to conserve energy and allow for life to resume if and when the threat goes away.

What happens in civilized life

In the natural environment in which we evolved, dangers were of such nature that Fight-Flight was an appropriate response. In civilized life, the nature of the threats is such that the Fight-or-Flight circuit is often inadequate.

Let's take an elementary example. If your coworkers are annoying you, it's usually not a good idea to punch them or run away from them. The energy generated by the Fight-or-Flight circuit has no place to go.

In the state of nature, the Fight-Flight energy was released by being utilized. In the civilized world, this energy stays with us in a very uncomfortable and toxic way. This is what is known as stress.

We do not find it easy to release it. And so, it has lasting emotional and physiological effects. There is a lingering, cumulative quality to the stress. An analogy can help explain why a quality that is useful under natural conditions turns out to be a big problem in civilized life. Think about our ability to store fat. It was a great resource when we lived under conditions where we could not count on a steady food supply. But in civilized life, we keep storing food without using the reserves we had saved, which has harmful consequences. Similarly, the Fight-Flight energy was meant to be consumed quickly in dealing with the threat, not stored in a way that ends up being detrimental to us.

What about the third circuit of the autonomous nervous system, the Shutdown circuit? It is triggered under extreme circumstances where the Fight-Flight circuit is unable to deal with the threat. In the environment where our remote ancestors lived, these were truly extreme conditions.

The Fight-Flight circuit and the energy it brought were appropriate for the vast majority of threatening situations that our ancestors faced. The shutdown or collapse was the exception rather than the norm. Not so in the civilized world. The Fight-Flight circuit is often not appropriate for dealing with situations.

So, while the situations themselves are not life-or-death situations, our organism perceives them as such because the Fight-Flight circuit cannot deal with them. And we automatically shift to the Shutdown circuit. We experience ourselves as confronting an overwhelming threat.

It is essential to remember that these are not conscious decisions but automatic reactions in the presence of a threat.

How we experience the three circuits

Which circuit is activated colors the experience we have of the situation. Under the Mindful Engagement circuit, we perceive the situation as challenging but manageable. In Fight-Flight mode, there is a heightened intensity and urgency. We have a sense that we're fighting for our lives or running away to save our lives. In Shutdown mode, we feel that all resistance is futile. We collapse or disengage. This is not a conscious decision to disengage but an automatic shift into the more primitive survival circuit.

In the following paragraphs, I will go into more detail.

Being in Mindful Engagement mode is essentially like being a fish in the water. As the expression goes, things go swimmingly. We are in harmony with our environment. It feels good, so we are drawn to this state. We naturally go toward what feels good and away from what feels bad.

Being in Fight-Flight mode does not feel good, but the point then is not to feel good. It is to face a significant danger and survive. Under natural conditions, once the threat is gone, our energy is spent. We return to a state where we're feeling in balance and harmony with our surroundings.

It is normal for us to face threats. We have a capacity for resilience, which means overcoming the negative effect of that high-level activation. Another way to describe resilience would be to talk about it as plasticity, the ability to go back to normal after a spike. In a state of nature, the threat usually comes to an end. The gazelle runs away from the lion. If it successfully escapes, the danger is over, and the gazelle can relax. There is no residual Fight-Flight energy, as it was used up in the flight.

However, in civilized life, that extra energy is often not fully discharged. There are many threats. And not all of them are easily managed through Fight-Flight. So, there is a residual impact of stress.

If stress is not fully discharged, we are not just reacting to the present moment. We are responding to the accumulated stress. Or to the way we perceive the present moment through our memories.

To put it another way: In the natural environment we evolved in, we could be living in Mindful Engagement mode much of the time, with spikes in Fight-Flight for specific threats, coming back down to Mindful Engagement soon afterward. In the civilized world, we live with the cumulative effect of past activation.

The experience of activation

What is the experience of being in states of ongoing activation?

When we are not in Mindful Engagement mode for extended periods, we do not have the stability, the resting place, where we can get our bearings. Life, as we experience it in Fight-Flight mode, is a constant struggle. The emotional landscape is one of ups and downs, inherently chaotic. In Shutdown mode, the experience is that of collapsing ("what's the point?") or being disengaged from life, living like a zombie—life as a living dead.

Instead of the fluid experience of returning to Mindful Engagement after a crisis, we cycle between Fight-Flight and Shutdown. We experience bursts of frantic, chaotic activity alternating and collapse or shutdown as this activity feels hopeless.

Saying that it does not feel good is an understatement. It feels unbearable. We strive for a sense of balance, of harmony—a sense of feeling OK. We instinctively try to get to some sense of feeling OK. This is how we cling on to coping mechanisms, i.e., whatever makes this suffering less unbearable.

Coping mechanisms

Coping mechanisms alleviate suffering. But they are far from perfect solutions. They do not deal with the underlying problems, and they take a toll. Addiction is one such coping mechanism. It is an attempt to solve the situation. It is a way of medicating the pain, of feeling some reprieve, at least temporarily. Unfortunately, the cost is high, not just in terms of having side effects, but also because, ultimately, it doesn't solve the underlying problem. Instead, it creates a cycle in which you feel temporary relief, then the after-effects, which include feeling ashamed. This draws you further into the cycle. Addiction becomes a problem of its own, beyond whatever situation might have triggered it initially.

In a broader perspective, coping mechanisms include things that we would not ordinarily put in the same category as addictions. These are patterns we develop when we find it impossible to find the sense of harmony that comes from feeling like a fish in the water. When we cannot shift back to Mindful Engagement, we build a pseudo self that gives us the illusion of that feeling.

We find some degree of harmony with the world by creating a different way of interacting with it. For instance, to counteract the scary sense of uncertainty, we hang on to some fixed beliefs or behaviors. It may be an addiction. It may also be a rigid ideology. Or rigid patterns, such as being always nice or always smiling. We are hanging on to a rigid shell in an attempt to experience some sense of permanence and safety.

It is essential to keep in mind the complexity and intricacy of what is at play. It is not just that traumatic stress causes us to hang on to coping mechanisms. There is a bi-directional effect. As we use our coping mechanisms, we reinforce the conditioned learning that we cannot handle difficult situations without these coping mechanisms. In doing so, we support a pattern of learned helplessness, i.e., we reinforce the traumatic stress itself.

Trying to force out the coping mechanism leaves you without any protection whatsoever against something excruciatingly difficult. No wonder it doesn't work.

It is more effective to think of this within the context of how the organism reacts to threat. Not threat as a temporary situation, but a lasting, ongoing threat that becomes the very fabric of life.

Because of the intricacies described earlier, the healing process is not linear. It is more of a dance in which things come progressively into focus.

The healing process

The following describes how the arc of the Proactive Twelve Steps dovetails with the healing process.

The process starts with an acknowledgment of the threat that is inherent in the situation: "I am not able to control what I do, and this has serious consequences" (Step 1). A significant threat is looming over you. You have no control over it because you have no control over yourself.

In terms of the nervous system, it means you are in Fight-Flight mode or Shutdown mode or cycling between them. So you are not able to come back to Mindful Engagement mode fluidly.

Then, with Steps 2 and 3 comes the defining intuition of what this process is about: finding in yourself a calm and patient way of being, i.e., the Mindful Engagement mode.

Keep in mind that this is not a linear process. Step 2 is not akin to crossing a threshold to enter a house. It is not a clear-cut change; it is a process.

The big change is not happening right away -- and yet, in some way, it is. For instance, take Step 3, taking a pause, moment by moment. Pausing does not change problematic attitudes and behaviors. And yet, something is happening. Taking that pause is a different way of being than being caught in the middle of the cycle. You are starting to be in Mindful Engagement mode.

Then, Steps 4 through 10 describe in more detail the dance of making the changes happen. The word "dance" captures the quality of interaction that is inherent in this process.

It's not as simple as "Just do it." It takes proceeding step by step. You are learning from experience as you encounter various obstacles that appear as you move along.

It is not just a cognitive learning process. You are progressively training your nervous system to classify the threats as manageable and thus be less reactive.

Step 4 refers to paying attention to your patterns of relating to people and situations. It means seeing the pseudo-self that you have unconsciously constructed to experience some stability in a confusing, chaotic, and uncontrollable world.

Step 5 corresponds to a profound desire to understand what is happening. It involves self-empathy, reinforced by the healing experience of having another person compassionately listening to you. Think of it in terms of nervous activation coming down, settling into Mindful Engagement mode as you experience connection.

With Mindful Engagement comes greater understanding. That's how, in Step 6, you can see that these patterns have been coping mechanisms. As you take the measure of the suffering, you also understand better why coping mechanisms would arise.

You then get in touch with the intensity of the fears and vulnerability that push you to have coping mechanisms (Step 7).

Because coping mechanisms serve to stave off profound fears, it is impossible to change them through willpower alone (as in "Just do it"). This is why it is important to proceed carefully, deliberately, and try these new mindful behaviors while you feel safe. That's why Step 8 involves rehearsing.

After you gain some confidence in these new patterns and have practiced them enough, they start to feel less foreign to you. It is now possible to apply them in everyday life, which is Step 9. And, in Mindful Engagement mode, you can do what you could not have done before: sincerely apologize to people you had hurt.

As you have a deeper understanding of how your coping mechanisms are related to your fears, you know that you cannot take your new habits for granted. You are aware that fear could quickly bring them back. This is why you keep paying attention to the causes and effects of your actions. That's Step 10.

Having gone through this lengthy process, you have come to understand that it takes intentionality to shift to Mindful Engagement mode. So, you make space for mindful reflection. Being in Mindful Engagement mode means you are naturally in touch with a felt sense of meaning and purpose. That's Step 11.

And so, by Step 12, you have come to understand at a deep level that it's not easy being human. And you have a growing sense of respect and compassion for yourself and others.

Finding safety in connection

As can be seen in this broad sweep, these steps are not separate. Instead, they are parts of a complex process of transformation.

In particular, you can better understand why Steps 4 through 10 seem to be proceeding so slowly, with what appears like tiny differences between steps. It is because these steps describe what it takes to foster a fundamental shift in the nervous system. That is a shift from the two more primitive circuits to the more sophisticated Mindful Engagement circuit, also known as the social Engagement circuit.

In the presence of a significant threat (or perceived threat), you cannot force yourself to override powerful survival mechanisms honed by eons of evolution. It takes progressive learning and fine-tuning for our nervous system to experience a sense of safety that makes it possible to release the more primitive safety mechanisms.

It takes a slow and deliberate approach to turn the overwhelming threat into threats that the Mindful Engagement circuit can manage. There is a dance: this circuit gets more engaged as you progressively engage with the situation and gain control of it.

Through this process, you find safety in connection through progressive engagement, allowing fears to lift organically as the sense of safety increases.

Part 4:
A spiritual & philosophical context

Having a spiritual or a philosophical outlook does not necessarily mean that you are a card-carrying member of a particular religion or philosophy. It might mean that you have some sense of how things fit together and how you fit in it. For most of us, this is not at all a crystal-clear vision. it is more like a vague sense, one that varies moment by moment. It might be a felt sense of being part of something larger. Or a felt sense of meaning and purpose. It is not something that could be crisply articulated, like a mission statement. It is more like a general sense that feels right, even though it might be challenging to describe what makes it so.

Exploring these issues is not the same thing as preaching a sermon or writing an academic paper. You don't have to convince anybody by trying to make clear what is fuzzy. Let your curiosity guide you. What you come up with need not fit in any pre-ordained category.

Agnostics and atheists in a God environment

What is it like to be in a program where God or some form of Higher Power plays a significant role if you don't relate to these notions? I have asked this question to agnostics and atheists who are very invested in the Twelve Steps. Here are some of their statements.

Please note that these are not people who stay away from Twelve Step programs because they are uncomfortable about the spiritual beliefs. These people are committed to the program they are in and gratefully acknowledge how helpful it has been. But, even after many years of successful participation in a program, the spiritual issue remains troubling.

Am I supposed to believe in a concept of God? Or is it more myself that I believe in? And that's where I'm struggling. Is the proof in me? Also, the language to use. If I say "Mother Earth" instead of God, people are going to look at me like I'm a lunatic.

- - -

I would never put the 12 step programs down because AA has gotten millions of people sober. And, during the pandemic, I have been attending an ACA meeting at least once a day. I don't feel right about looking for somebody else outside of me. So, when I go to meetings, I basically don't talk.

- - -

I'm a member of Narcotics Anonymous. I've been abstinent for a long time. But there is the Higher Power piece. It is something that I... I don't want to use the word struggle, but... it hasn't made sense to me. I'm having a hard time because I consider myself an atheist, and that doesn't always fit in a 12-step fellowship.

- - -

Over the years, I have found myself sharing a little more about this type of thing [not believing in God]. I feel like I'm making some sort of confession, that I don't believe like you guys might believe, or like our literature says we're supposed to believe.

- - -

Missing out

There can be a lingering feeling that, somehow, you haven't quite gotten it right. That, maybe, you are missing out on something important.

- - -

I've been abstinent for a long time. And I still haven't figured this out. Like I should have figured this out by now. Like, why haven't I gotten this? You know, why do I not believe? I hear other people share, and they seem to have such a grasp on it.

- - -

They all sort of say the same thing, that there's something there that they just feel. And that's where I think, well, am I supposed to be feeling it? Is this a lack of confidence in myself that I'm not feeling something? A connection from somewhere greater than me? So I put pressure on myself. I start spinning on all this other stuff. I tell myself, you're missing something. There's something, they have something that you don't have, or they see something that you don't see.

- - -

I'm willing, you know, I have a lot of willingness, but it's that sort of direct line to something outside, where I get stuck. I'm trying to find a way not to be stuck, not to feel stuck. I want to be okay with exactly how I feel on any given day, but, you know, that's a lot to ask.

- - -

A sense of pressure

Some people experience a sense of pressure. Not necessarily overt pressure, but some sense of condescension or dismissal.

- - -

I've worked through the steps, and they've changed my life. It's become a kind of a template for how I conduct myself in the world. But I still find that I get that pit in my stomach when I share about this stuff like I might be saying something that I'm not supposed to say. And I might alter what I'm saying, or I might not exactly say exactly how I feel because I don't want people to judge me. I don't want them to say, or feel; you don't belong here because you don't follow things exactly. And that's dramatic, but that's how I feel inside, right?

- - -

There's a bit of intimidation because some people, if you say it's me and my actions, would say, oh, but you're arrogant. You need to turn over to God. You turn over to a higher power. And so there's that sense that you didn't get it.

- - -

Internal pressure

The pressure is not necessarily coming from others in the group exercising overt pressure. Much of it might be internal rather than external.

- - -

I'm my own biggest enemy in this. I don't have anyone in my life telling me that I have to believe anything. I do this to myself.

- - -

There's a piece of me that wants to believe, that wants to be like those people, you know? I hear them talk about how things can be so much easier. I get all wrapped up in myself. And I sometimes think if I had that turning it over ability, I wouldn't get so tight in my chest when I think about certain things. I wouldn't get that sick feeling. I'd be able to say, God's got it. And, I don't have that.

- - -

If I'm sitting in a room full of people, there's the part of me that's individualistic. And also the part of me that knows privately that I need to belong. It is probably not true anymore that I need to, but I can still get that primal urge, that I'm going to die if I don't believe as they believe.

Authentic

What feels especially sad is that the programs are meant to free you, to help you find a more authentic way to live.

- - -

I am a member of a 12-step fellowship. I have been in recovery for a long time. The words they have, they're not expressing what I mean. I want to find words that work for me to describe my beliefs without having to twist words that I hear in the fellowship. I'm doing the word substitution real quick in my head. I don't like that. It's like I go along to get along. And that doesn't feel right. In recovery, we strive to be authentic, and that doesn't feel authentic to me. It's supposed to be authentic, and the whole point is to be yourself. And, if you have to contort yourself, to confirm, you're doing something that doesn't quite fit.

- - -

When you feel that your beliefs are something that you have to dance around to be accepted, you are in a co-dependent mode with the group that is supposed to nurture you. You are caving in to old patterns of codependency within the program that is helping you overcome them.

- - -

It's not a question of imposing my beliefs on people but of standing up for my beliefs that are not quite covered by this language. I would appreciate having a little bit of room for finding a way to express who I am and what I believe in.

Expressing yourself

So, the issue of God is not just a spiritual or philosophical question. It's about being who you are and how you can forge a relationship with the group without losing yourself. What is needed is a renegotiation of your relationship with others on the basis of mutual respect. Here are some possible ways to express yourself.

Please do not take the following examples as statements that you need to memorize and deliver to the group you are in. Think of them as inspiration to ask yourself what it is you'd like to express. The goal is to reclaim your right to be who you are. You have your views. You have the right to be part of this community, even though you don't necessarily share all of their ideas.

You will grow by finding a way to negotiate your relationship with the group around what is important to you.

Let me suggest some ways of putting this into words. Not perfect words that you should memorize. Just an example to inspire you to come up with what feels right for you to say.

- - -

You, the group, you have something to give me that I value. But I want to get it while respecting myself and being respected for who I am. I don't want to lose myself to get accepted or lose the group if I state what's important to me.

- - -

I have a confession to make. I'm not feeling any pressure from you guys. This is an internal thing. I want to expose that part of me where I have this internal pressure that says, what you believe is not right. I'm here in a group where people commit to being nonjudgmental. So I'm going to take the risk to expose that part of myself.

- - -

I value this group. I value the program. I've internalized it. It has done lots of good things for me. And I want to confess that I'm a little bit shy about standing up for the fact that the word God or Higher Power doesn't quite reflect how I feel. And I don't have exact words to describe how I feel about my beliefs. I know that it doesn't quite feel right to use the words God or Higher Power. I certainly appreciate that something is happening, but I'm uncomfortable using these words.

- - -

The connection with a Higher Power is not part of my experience. I'm curious about it. Sometimes, I am worried about not having it. But it's not like I can only grasp material things. I feel very connected to people. I feel very good about being in this group. I would appreciate it if you don't push too much to teach me that connection to God as if I will not function well without it. I would like you to respect my doing what I do in my own way and at my own pace.

Higher Power & Inner Power

The Twelve Steps of A.A. refer to God and to "a power greater than ourselves." Why remove any mention of God or a Higher Power in these Proactive Steps?

One reason is that a secular approach is more likely to be understood by people who do not believe in God or a Higher Power. It's a good reason. But, if it were the only reason, it would be a very weak one. These Proactive Twelve Steps would only be some "lite" version of the "real" steps, and they would only be relevant to those people who "can't stomach the real thing."

Digging deeper into the process

I have found in rewriting the steps that eliminating God led me to pay more attention to describing the process. I alluded to this in the introduction. As we are further along in the process, this is an opportune time to dig deeper.

The essence of the Twelve Steps approach is to take your focus away from a specific problem that seems unmanageable. You shift your focus to another dimension. This powerful shift is like the "jump into hyperspace" in science-fiction movies.

In traditional Twelve Steps lore, this other dimension is described as "letting God" (or a Higher Power) guide you.

In the Proactive Twelve Steps, the "other dimension" consists of the process of living more mindfully. You mindfully pay attention to what you do, moment by moment. Little by little, you change your database of information. It means that you change the way your nervous system is wired. It also means that you change your sense of who you are.

As you change your sense of who you are, you deal with the intractable problems differently. The result feels nothing short of miraculous.

So, it is understandable that people would think of it as a miraculous intervention from a benevolent God.

Experience vs. concepts

It is good to keep in mind that there is a difference between what you experience and how you capture this experience in words. This is especially true when using religious or philosophical terms. It is easy to get pulled into arguing about the concepts and lose track of the fact that the actual experiences you are referring to may not be that far apart.

Instead of arguing about beliefs, such as whether or not there is a God, I suggest you focus on the experience itself. You are much more likely to find convergence this way. I'm going to give you examples of how to find convergence.

Some specifics

If you don't believe in God, you don't need to argue about that when you talk to somebody who does. Of course, you also don't need to force yourself to believe; it doesn't work. Focus on what is meaningful to you and talk about it in terms of what you experience.

Let's say you're in a support group, and you hear people talk about their experience of God. You might feel like you're missing out on something important. Don't focus on what you cannot feel. Instead, ask yourself what sustains you.

It might then dawn on you that being in this support group is what sustains you, what gives you motivation and strength. Bingo.

For you, being in a safe and compassionate group is a powerful experience. It feels like it brings people to a higher level of functioning than when they are alone.

So that is your experience of a higher power. It is not a thing, or a person, or a being. It is what happens in certain circumstances, e.g., being with kindred spirits. And you can share this with people: "When I am in this group, I have the experience of being part of something powerful."

If you are religious, I suggest you pay attention to your experience instead of just seeing it through the filter of spiritual concepts. This does not negate the spiritual ideas, and you may find that it enriches your spiritual outlook.

Convergence

I hope that these Proactive Twelve Steps help people with different belief systems get closer to a convergence of views. In the process I describe, you progressively get a sense that there is more to you than your "little ego," that is, the fear-driven, grasping part of you. As you gain the strength to overcome dysfunctional habits, your sense of self grows into something larger and more solid. You experience yourself as more connected to others as well as your deepest needs.

You can think of it as a power granted to you by an external Higher Power, e.g., God. Or you can think of it as an Inner Power that is part of human nature, something that you are getting better at tapping into. The philosophical context is different, but the underlying experience is very much the same.

I suggest you use the language of Inner Power, as it sticks more closely to the experience itself. The language of experience points to a common ground for people who are religious as well as people who are atheistic or agnostic. Having some common ground makes it possible to learn from each other's experiences instead of fighting over the cultural context.

Faith in human nature

When you hear the word faith, you probably think about religious belief. Or maybe, faith in God, not necessarily to a given religion.

Instead, I will be talking about the human capacity for the experience of faith, which has nothing to do with any specific belief system.

A human trait

It is a human characteristic that we all share. And faith healing is not just religious healing. How else would you explain the placebo effect?

A placebo is a little pill that has no chemical effect on the body. It is used as a 'control' in testing other medications. New medications are tested against a placebo to see whether they have any healing power beyond the placebo effect.

Faith is what makes it possible for an innocuous pill to have healing power?

It is the context. In this case, it is faith in doctors, science, the whole ideological superstructure of our civilization that we essentially trust to have the power to heal us. It works because we believe in it. Not in the pill per se, but in what it represents. Very much like the communion wafer for a Christian.

In other words: you don't have to be religious to experience the healing power of faith.

A down-to-earth perspective

This perspective is different from the conception in which faith entails some mystical connection to the transpersonal, to something beyond us.

Instead, I have a more down-to-earth perspective. I want to use the word "faith" in a much more limited sense, in the same way as we would use the word "trust."

Let's say, for instance, that you have a car that you have been using during a frigid winter. On a given day, as the weather forecast predicts a freezing day, you feel confident that your car will work. It doesn't even occur to you that it might not. You have faith in the car.

As something has repeatedly worked for you in the past, you trust that it will again. If friends have been there for you when things were hard, you probably assume that they will be there for you when things go wrong in the future. Suppose you have generally had luck under challenging circumstances. In that case, you are likely to have faith that you will be lucky in the future.

Let's go even further back in the past, back to your childhood. Suppose your parents were reliable support for you. In that case, you are more likely to feel that you live in a benevolent universe. If not, you might be more predisposed to seeing the world as harsh and unpredictable.

I am talking about how our various life experiences constitute a database of knowledge from which we implicitly project how we perceive the world. It is impossible for you, or me, or any human being, to discount the emotional impact that our previous experiences play in how we see the future. Human beings are amazingly good at learning. We learn from experience, and this is what colors our perception of the present and the future.

How does this help in a practical way?

Our tendency to trust in the future (or not) correlates with the experiences we have had in the past. When we remember this, we can consciously address our unconscious biases.

For one thing, it does not make sense to say: "I should have faith." You cannot force yourself to change whether or not you have faith because it reflects your experience. So it works better to accept that having faith (or not) is a given.

It is liberating to accept this instead of forcing yourself to be something you cannot be. You cannot change the past, but you can try to change your experiences in the present and the future.

What is it like in practice? Under challenging circumstances, you find yourself noticing your lack of faith in the future. Then you remember that it makes sense for you not to have faith given the database of experience that you've had in your life. Having acknowledged that, you can then be on the lookout for other facts. Other perspectives may then open up. You may see the current situation in a fresh way, not colored by baggage from the past.

Blind faith vs. building trust

We are not talking about trying to have blind faith in the future. We are talking about the possibility of building trust.

When we talk about building trust, it's something that happens in everyday life. In big things as well as in small things, you don't have to trust everybody blindly. That might be a pretty lousy life strategy - better concentrate on exploring whether it is possible to build trust.

To do this, you need to focus on what might be a foundation on which you can build trust and, over time, faith.

An excellent place to start is to keep asking yourself: "What is good in my life?" If this question is difficult for you, then: "What is it that is relatively less bad in my life?"

In so doing, you keep refocusing on what is reliable. Remember: unless something is solid, it's hard to build on it. You cannot build a house on quicksand. Bedrock will give you a better foundation.

You keep looking for what you can trust. You are not pretending that everything in your life is reliable. It's just that you are committed to focusing on what is working rather than what is not.

A metaphor

The image that comes to mind is: You're in the woods, and you have to cross a spring. It's too wide for you to jump over it. But there are big stones in the spring. You're going to put one foot on a rock and then one on the next rock, and so on until you get to the other side of the spring.

This metaphor applies to life. There is plenty of water, i.e., unpleasantness and danger. You know it, but you keep your focus on the rocks because that's what gets you where you want to go. As you do this, you build trust. You have faith, not because of some transcendent belief, but as the natural result of positive experiences.

Appendix 1:
The Proactive Twelve Steps

Step 1: I face reality. I am not able to control what I do, and this has serious consequences.

Step 2: I understand that I cannot force change through willpower. I need to disentangle my life patiently.

Step 3: Moment by moment, I take a mindful pause to deal with my life calmly and effectively.

Step 4: I examine my life with honesty, searching for patterns in how I have been relating to people and situations.

Step 5: I explore these patterns and describe them to another person, noticing the healing power of compassionate listening.

Step 6: I understand how these patterns have been ways of coping with my fears.

Step 7: I learn to accept the sense of vulnerability that goes with life's pressures and uncertainties.

Step 8: I explore alternative behaviors and rehearse them in safe settings.

Step 9: I apply these new mindful behaviors in my everyday life. I sincerely apologize to people I have hurt, except when counterproductive.

Step 10: I keep paying attention to the causes and effects of my actions. I act accordingly.

Step 11: I make space in my life for mindful reflection. A sense of meaning and purpose naturally arises from that.

Step 12: My life reflects a growing sense of respect and compassion for myself and others. I share this process with others who are struggling.

Appendix 2:

How to share this process with a friend or a group

How to structure the sessions

I highly recommend that you go through this program with a friend or a group of friends.

If you and your friends are familiar with Twelve Step groups, you can use the traditional structure.

If you're not familiar with that structure, or if you'd like to try something new, here is a structure that I recommend. It relies on Active Listening. It is a way to create a safe and respectful space that makes it possible for you to feel heard and gives you room for self-discovery.

Unlike therapy or coaching, there is no leader. You are among peers. Following an agreed-upon format gives your gathering a structure that is clear and avoids ambiguity. You are sharing experiences as peers, not giving or receiving advice.

The overall structure

You can get together in person, online, or by phone. I suggest you commit to fourteen sessions together, meeting once a week. You can space out the sessions more, but I suggest you don't have them more often than once a week. This way, you give yourselves time to digest each Step before moving to the next one.

Why fourteen sessions? In the first one, you go over the format together. You also share your hopes and fears about this process.

You can understand why it makes sense to share your hopes: It allows you to formulate them clearly and understand what everybody wants.

Sharing your fears is just as important. It is an excellent way to establish safety. It is virtually impossible not to be somewhat scared as you embark on an exploration of complex issues. Acknowledging the fears and committing to safety and respect will go a long way toward making this process more productive.

The following twelve session are each devoted to one step. I will go through the structure of a session in more detail below.

The last session is one in which you reflect on the process: What you have learned about yourself. What has changed? What has not changed? What do you want to focus on in the future?

It is also an excellent time to discuss whether or not you want to continue to meet beyond the initial fourteen sessions. If you continue, there are several ways that you can do it:
- One option is to do another round of the Proactive Twelve Steps, revisiting them in light of the experience you have gained during this first round.
- Another is to have ongoing regular meetings where you can talk about the challenges of your life. You do this with the same Active Listening format, i.e., there is no advice given or taken. The goal is for each of you to have space to hear yourself think.
- You can also choose to have meetings devoted to talking about other chapters of this book. This

discussion, too, takes place under the same format, talking about your experiences in such a way that you can hear yourself think, with no advice given or taken.

The structure of a session

Let's say that each session lasts about an hour. You can make the session shorter if there are just two of you or longer if there are several of you.

I invite you to open each session with a short moment of silence (a minute or two).

Then, one person reads the Step that you are exploring that day. I suggest you rotate who does it.

Then comes the sharing. Count on ten to twenty minutes of sharing per person. I will describe the Active Listening format below.

After everybody has shared, allow a little time for people to reflect on the process itself. That is, what people found helpful (or unhelpful) in the sharing and how they were being listened to. This kind of feedback helps you be better attuned to others' needs and your own needs. Plan on a few minutes per person, at least in the first few sessions.

At the end of the session, keep a few minutes for a very brief "bookmark." Each participant finds a word or two, or an image, to remember what came up for them.

Active Listening

I will now describe Active Listening. When you first try it, you will likely feel a little awkward. This feeling is normal because it's different from what you're accustomed to. After you try it, you will probably appreciate the result. Here are a few pointers on how to do it.

In the following, I will describe the process as if there were only two of you, in which case you alternate being Talker and Listener. If there are more of you, it is easy to adapt. For instance, if there are 3 of you:
- First, A is the Talker, and B is the Listener. C witnesses in silence.
- Then B is the Talker, and C the Listener. A witnesses in silence.
- Finally, C is the Talker, and A the Listener. B witnesses in silence.

Taking turns

A defining feature of Active Listening is that the two of you take turns, one being the Talker while the other is the Listener. And then you switch.

In ordinary life, we tend to multitask. That is, we prepare our arguments while we are listening. This approach might work well enough in everyday conversations, but it is not enough when there is more emotional content.

It takes a deliberate plan to override the usual way we function. For instance, if you're going to be talking for half an hour, you decide that one of you will be the Talker for the first 15 minutes, and the other will be the Talker for the next 15 minutes. An effortless way to avoid any feelings about who starts is to toss a coin.

Focus on understanding

Another defining feature of Active Listening is that the Listener focuses on trying to understand the Talker. Keep in mind that understanding somebody does not mean giving up your own opinion. As the Listener, you are just trying to understand the Talker's point of view from their point of view. You don't have to agree.

Summarizing

The third characteristic of Active Listening is that, as the Listener, you give the Talker a summary of what you've heard. You don't wait until the full 15 or 20 minutes to do that. You do it every couple of minutes. Sometimes it could be just a minute or so. There's a natural rhythm that the two of you develop over time.

Taking it in

The fourth characteristic is that the Talker pays attention to the summary and takes it in. The Talker either nods in approval, says yes, or amends it by adding something that the Listener did not pick up.

By the way, it's OK if the Talker adds something to what you, the Listener, have said. Very often, this helps the Talker better understand what it is that was important to them.

So, either way: either the Talker keeps nodding to what you're saying, or it's an opportunity for them to find something else. In both cases, it's fine. And you continue this way: talking, listening, summarizing, taking it in, until the end of the allotted time for the Talker. Then, you switch.

Pausing and making space

The fifth characteristic of Active Listening is that it involves pausing. This is not a rapid-fire, yackety yack, type of conversation. Both the Talker and the Listener are engaged in making space. It is what allows the new, the unformed, to come up.

As the Listener, you pause before giving your summary to the Talker. You don't jump in with your summary as soon as the Talker pauses. You give them a chance because maybe they're just waiting to say something more.

As the Talker, don't feel like you have to fill the air with words. It's OK if you take time without words while you're trying to sense what comes up next. Let yourself be curious about the felt sense of it. In other words, be prepared that much of what comes up may be murky. It's not a problem. It's actually a good thing. "Murky" is an invitation to explore further, as opposed to "case closed."

What about advice?

One thing is missing from these instructions: how to give advice. For a simple reason: you neither give nor receive advice.

Remember that this is a peer group. You are together to help each other find space to hear yourself think.

As you read this, it probably seems obvious. However, sooner or later, as you get involved in the process, there will come a moment when you find it unbearable not to give advice. Why let this person suffer needlessly when you could so quickly tell them what to do? Not all the time, but just this once, when it would be so easy and so helpful!

When that time comes, and it will, please remember to take a deep breath and resist the urge. You are not failing the other person by refraining from giving advice. You are helping them be face to face with what they need to face.

You might be reading a degree of suffering on the other person's face. At such a time, what I call "spaciousness" in this description of the process probably feels like terrifying emptiness to the person you are listening to.

I am not asking you to be heartless, just to express your compassion differently. Keep in mind that, by being present, you make it easier for the other person to confront this void than if they were on their own. You may want to express your support by making small sounds, showing that you are present.

You don't have to do it right

A final point about Active Listening is that you don't have to do it right. The format encourages thoughtful give-and-take as part of the process. Over time, the two of you will learn, by trial and error, better ways to do Active Listening.

Appendix 3:

From self-control to co-regulation: A conversation with neuroscientist Stephen Porges

This journey of self-discovery starts with the realization that "I am not able to control what I do" in Step 1. It would seem that the solution is to develop self-control. Unfortunately, attempts to do this prove to be futile. Step 2 is the realization that "I understand that I cannot force change through willpower."

Getting there involves a significant shift in how you view what it's like to be a human being. Our culture still reflects assumptions that have been disproved by neuroscience and evolutionary psychology.

The traditional perspective values self-control as the ability to keep impulses in check. It views this struggle in moralistic terms: The sense that it is good to pull yourself up by your bootstraps.

Of course, it makes sense to put a high value on our efforts to face adversity. But the danger is that it fosters an unrealistic idea of what it's like to be a human being. Essentially, we are social animals. Our interactions shape us. This is a core insight of the Twelve Steps, as nine of the steps have to do with social interactions.

The following conversation with Stephen Porges is not about the Twelve Steps. It is about the perspective on what it's like to be human that he developed in his work as a neuroscientist. It has been a profound inspiration in my professional work as well as in writing this book.

Stephen W. Porges, Ph.D., is Distinguished University Scientist at Indiana University, where he directs the Trauma Research Center within the Kinsey Institute. He holds the position of Professor of

Psychiatry at the University of North Carolina and Professor Emeritus at the University of Illinois at Chicago and the University of Maryland.

He served as president of both the Society for Psychophysiological Research and the Federation of Associations in Behavioral & Brain Sciences and is a former recipient of a National Institute of Mental Health Research Scientist Development Award.

In 1994 he proposed the Polyvagal Theory, a theory that links the evolution of the mammalian autonomic nervous system to social behavior and emphasizes the importance of physiological state in the expression of behavioral problems and psychiatric disorders.

The following are four excerpts from this conversation.

Self in interaction

Serge: Focusing on "me" as a separate person is like imagining that a person could exist without an environment.

Stephen: Human life starts with the parent and the child, with the child being regulated by the parent. The child's implicit visceral feelings are being contained or structured in a way as not to be too chaotic or disrupted. Tantrums are ameliorated.

Serge: So, whenever we talk about "self-regulation", we miss the boat.

Stephen: We miss the boat.

Serge: And "co-regulation" or "interface" or things like that have more to do with the reality of the process.

Stephen: Our biology defines many of our attributes, including our vulnerabilities. There's an overall paradox. The individuals who appear to be efficient in regulating themselves are the ones who have had more opportunities to effectively co-regulate with others. Their nervous system has a history of neural exercise that would promote resilience.

The traditional model of resilience was that if an individual was supported too much, the experience of support would compromise the individual's ability to take care of themselves. I believe this a misunderstanding of the needs of humans.

Humans need to be co-regulated because the experience of being co-regulated develops resilience. This will enable a human to self-regulate when it is not possible to co-regulate.

Serge: The old model was that adversity is good for you; it builds character. The transition was to talk about regulation - - as in "we're teaching you something, which is how to regulate." But what is being taught is the ability to interface.

Stephen: Right. The success of the interface is seen in the bodily response. When the body becomes more physiologically regulated, it is calmer. This physiological state promotes opportunities to feel safe and to develop trusting relationships. An added bonus is that a history of successful and predictable co-regulation tunes the nervous system to be sufficiently resilient to function during periods of separation. It's almost as if it's a paradox. But, as a therapist, you can see what happens when those experiences early in life are not met. When people are not co-regulated, their ability to self-regulate is severely compromised, and their behavior can be disruptive.

Serge: Yes. Because self-regulation does not exist by itself, we're talking about how we adapt to the environment, whether it's an actual environment or a perceived environment. In a way, it's about our interactions with threat.

Stephen: Right. From a clinical perspective, what is an important manifestation of many mental health disorders? It is the inability to co-regulate with another.

Trauma, abuse, and neglect result in difficulties in co-regulating. These difficulties are manifested in problems in establishing and maintaining good relationships.

A reliable portal to evaluating a person's successful adaptation – even their sense of fulfillment—is whether they co-regulate their physiology in the presence of others. The metaphor I love to use is that we need to feel safe in the arms of another appropriate mammal. Remember: some people co-regulate more effectively with their pets than with their spouses.

Serge: Right. So, essentially, it is to co-regulate in the presence of another mammal.

Stephen: Yes. At some point in their life, all mammals need to co-regulate. But social mammals, such as humans, need to co-regulate throughout their whole life. They start with their parents, then involve peers and significant others. The circle is completed when they become parents and are empowered with the role of co-regulating their children.

Serge: You notice the beauty of this: As we're talking about it in these terms, tasks like parenting become a little different. It's not "I'm going to teach the kids something" but "My being with my kids in a certain way is going to help them be that way."

Stephen: I agree. I use the word 'neural exercises' to emphasize that we need to exercise our social engagement system. If we don't, we have problems socially, mentally, and physically. These problems may become exacerbated as we get older. They may even be linked to accelerated aging.

The concept of a 'neural exercise' is different than learning. It's not learning through reinforcement, although the benefits may promote positive feelings. It is more dependent on what our nervous system craves. It craves social interactions that provide opportunities to co-regulate. And while co-regulating, the nervous system is better able to regulate physiological states to optimize health, growth, and restoration.

Our mental processes are simultaneously enhanced, and our thoughts can be bolder, more expansive and creative, and perhaps even spiritual. These emergent features are not going to be expressed if we're in the state of constant threat, if we're physiologically unable to co-regulate.

Serge: Again, this is about not focusing on the individual only. Instead, thinking that we exist as part of a context. That all of life exists that way. What we're talking about is finding the conditions under which certain capacities can expand and function optimally.

Stephen: Absolutely.

Embodied experience

Stephen: I do a little exercise in my workshops. I have people do it in pairs. They take ten relatively rapid inhalations and ten slow exhalations. Then they take ten long inhalations and ten rapid exhalations. I have them observe each other: they have an observer on one person's breathing, and then they reverse roles.

When people take longer inhalations and shorter exhalations, they see the person observing them as extraordinarily critical. They may say, "What did I do wrong? Why are you looking at me that way?" This occurs because they shifted their physiological state by breathing.

However, when they breathe with a longer and slower exhalation, they say, "Oh, what an attractive person. I like to know that person a little better."

It's an example of how something as simple as our breathing pattern can change our perspective of the person sitting across from us. It's an amazing phenomenon to watch and to hear comments like, "Wow, how did this happen?"

Serge: It's a beautiful example. The exercise shows how the way you breathe helps you shift. When you're slower, you're in a calmer place. You're feeling seen, feeling a sense of connection. With the faster exhalation, you experience the other person as critical and judgmental. This is a beautiful example of a physical inner state and its impact on how people perceive the situation.

Stephen: It's explainable. During exhalation, the impact of the vagus nerve on the heart becomes greater. A slow exhalation calms you down. With the breathing exercise, you can see this functioning in front of your eyes.

When you see an anxious person, you can see the person's anxiety in their breathing pattern. You will see fast short exhalations. Sometimes these breaths are very short and appear to be gasps. Breathing this way creates a physiological state that supports anxiety.

When you see someone getting angry, they're doing the same thing. They're shifting their breathing pattern to create a physiological state that supports the anger and the hostility.

Serge: The implication is to take emotions less seriously. Emotions are how we perceive the world. If I feel angry, or if I feel judged, I'm going to act on it. What you're saying is that experiencing the differences in breathing gives you a sense of how the emotion can be affected by how you process it.

Therefore, it's not an abstraction to say, "don't follow your emotions." Instead of just following the emotion, you can have a different experience of it. You don't have to oppose intellect with emotion, but you can process the emotion within a broader context.

Stephen: I play with these ideas, and I talk about it as shifting our personal narrative. When you have a physiological state that mobilizes you and gets you reactive, you develop a personal narrative that supports that you are at fault. "Not me; you are the bad person."

Your physiological state would drive this anger. If you shift your physiology to a calmer state, you wouldn't be reacting that way.

Serge: When you say "shifting," there's an active role. Instead of being a passive receptor of experience, and this experience then dictates what I do, I have a role in how I perceive my experience.

Stephen: I not only have a role, I can receive and shift my physiological state through a very primitive but voluntary manipulation: changing how I breathe. I use two types of processes. I'm talking about a passive pathway and an active pathway. The passive pathway involves the cues you may be signaling me, or I may be signaling you. The intonation of voice, facial expression, hand gesture, and body posture may contribute to the passive pathway. But the active pathway would be something like breathing which would come from an awareness of what my body is doing.

We tend to be unaware of the cues that shift our physiological state. But we are usually always aware of our physiological state shift. If we're aware of it, we can intercede. We can do something. We can take our body out of that place, or we can do a breathing exercise. We can respect what our body is doing and say, I don't need to create that narrative to justify that physiological state. I can see why that's happened. I reacted, and now I need to change my state so I can truly evaluate the situation.

Serge: The entry point is the awareness of the physiological experience. From that awareness of the physiological experience, there is the possibility of experimenting with it, of shifting it. Then, as you shift it, you experience yourself - - both yourself and the situation - - in a different way.

Stephen: Yes.

Serge: In a way, what you describe is very simple. You're saying, "Look. This is what you pay attention to. This is how you shift". This includes how you breathe. At the same time, it's a very deep concept, a way to answer the question of "Who am I?" It's the sense of, "I am at the interaction of these various things."

Stephen: Actually, it's a great question because who is the real you – are you the reactive person, or are you the calm person? Who is the real you. In a sense, we are both. And both are dependent on our implicit feelings – our physiological state. And, functionally, we act out. There is an implicit sense of hierarchy, which assumes that if we're not reactive to the intrusions, the 'real' person – loving and calm -can express him or herself.

Serge: When we put it that way: "Who are you? The calm person, or the reactive person?" these concepts seem to be static: You are this or that. The model that you're describing is actually experiencing oneself as a process.

Stephen: Dynamically adjusting and experiencing the self as it changes. As we shift physiological states, the shift in our physiology influences our awareness of ourselves. Once we are aware and respectful of these changes, we may experience a sense of self-compassion.

You start respecting and witnessing what you're doing, of basically who you are.

Serge: I want to highlight this. Self-compassion is often seen as a "good quality" or a "good attitude" with quote marks. But, as you're describing it, you are describing a process. The process of following reality moment by moment and playing and experimenting. This is in contrast to a sense of, "I want to be good and open and accepting." It's a different definition and one that is more humanly attainable.

Stephen: It's again linked to this respect of what the body actually is doing. It's not a cognitive construct superimposed on our bodily experience. It's allowing the body to respond and truly experience the body responses and have a degree of awareness. I'm going to use this term, respect for what the body is doing.

Serge: You're not saying, "the value is respect, and you have to force yourself to be respectful." But "I'm going to give you a pathway. If you follow the body experience, if you start to play with it and experiment with it and tinker with it in a certain way, you will start to have that perspective. You will have respect for who you are as a body".

Stephen: Right. What you are just talking about was very good for me to hear. It reminded me that people have different perspectives about what is "good" or not good regarding their bodily reactions. I'm not labeling the reactivity or the calmness as good or bad. I'm saying that you become aware of it. As you respect going through these stages, you can decide where you want to be.

Serge: We shifted from a notion of "what is good, what is bad" to the notion of process. That is a sense of being in that moment-by-moment process and that dance.

Stephen: Yes.

Serge: Being in the dance with oneself and seeing the complexities moment by moment will make it easier to see other people as more complex than simply cardboard cutouts.

Stephen: Right. Because part of our own body and body reaction is to connect and co-regulate with others, this dynamic interaction enables the other to regulate. As we regulate with them, it becomes a shared responsibility to co-regulate. We shift from the individual wanting something to the individual being dynamically involved in communicating with another individual.

Trauma, respect & shame

Serge: Take the case where you're in an extreme situation, a major threat. Say, there's a mob of angry people, and you're all alone. Are you going to be able to self-regulate? There's probably a built-in impossibility for that kind of regulation to function under certain conditions. You cannot do more than what you're capable of doing.

Stephen: Your body is going to evaluate the degree of risk. It's not going to be an explicit cognitive decision. Hopefully, if there's an angry mob of people coming towards you, your body will mobilize to ensure escape. However, sometimes, some individuals will be locked in an immobilized state of fear rather than escaping. This immobilization is not based on a conscious decision but a bodily reaction not under their control. The threshold to immobilize instead of escape may be related to earlier traumas or a history of abuse. They may have experienced in response to threat a behavioral shutdown or even passed out.

Their body 'reflexively' decided to immobilize outside of conscious awareness. A therapeutic strategy to deal with individuals who have similar experiences is to help them respect their body's decision and not criticize their body for deciding to immobilize.

Serge: We're talking again about that moment-by-moment experience where, to the extent possible, we're freed from the influence of trauma that blocks us from being really in the moment. Also, not presupposing that there is a right and a wrong answer. For instance, it's not like you should trust that goodness will triumph and openness and connection will triumph when facing the angry mob. You take appropriate action while being able to be present and have all the resources you have.

Stephen: The real clinical question relates to identifying the appropriate action. In your statement, the appropriate action would be implied in the degree of being present, which means being aware and in control of one's behavior. Some people's bodies will react with a different physiological response profile, which makes them more likely to engage in fight-flight behaviors, in contrast to shutting down. Similarly, the reaction to engage in fight-flight behaviors is not based on a conscious decision. In either case, we can't get angry at the body for what it has done. We have to understand it and respect it for what it has done.

Again, trauma-related immobilization is frequently experienced by people who have been molested or raped. These immobilization experiences are frequently re-lived by the survivors with feelings of guilt about not fighting or running. Instead of feeling guilt for an involuntary reaction to a threat, the client needs to create a personal narrative that incorporates an understanding of the evolutionary 'adaptive' advantages of immobilizing instead of fighting.

The client needs to be informed that, by immobilizing, they were less likely to be killed or to be injured.

Serge: The essential part I want to highlight here is we're talking about respecting the body. We're putting this in contrast to the experience of trauma and abuse, where the body is disrespected. There is learning about disrespecting or distrusting the body. We're making the point that it's crucial to respect the body and contrasting this with trauma.

Stephen: Even within trauma, the survivor must respect their own body's reaction and not be angry with their own body.

Serge: Yes. The survivor has to respect that the body has its limitations due to the trauma. But there is a complicating factor. The training in disrespect related to trauma means that it might be more difficult for the trauma victim to respect what you can do at that moment.

Stephen: Yes.

Serge: You emphasize the concept of respect. You are outlining a path for what it means and how to get to it, which is very experiential and process-oriented instead of an abstract notion.

Stephen: I agree.

Let's shift to another important and related concept, shame. If one respects their bodily reactions, then the experience of shame may be blunted. This is because shame is frequently experienced as a derivative of our interpretation of our own body's reaction.

Shame becomes an important element of the personal narrative, as the individual attempts to place meaning on their bodily feelings. Shame contributes to the personal narrative by using our higher brain structures to organize our body reactions and feelings. Thus, understanding and respecting bodily feelings becomes

important. A positive understanding of our feelings
helps us understand how we react to various situations.

*Serge: Yes. Respect vs. shame. Shame as lack of respect and
humiliation, "you're not okay." A very powerful pole of
human experience.*

Stephen: The shame is embedded in one's own body.
That leads to a lack of respect for the body. It's not
merely that the person was disrespected. It is that they
no longer respect their own body.

Personal narratives, safety & connection

Serge: We're talking about the difference between the experience of the bodily feelings and the language we superimpose over this experience, over these bodily feelings.

Stephen: That's where this concept of respect comes in. The body is going to respond, is going to react, is going to have feelings. The question is now, what do we do with those feelings. We understand that our body is doing what it can do because that's what it does. Gaining a more informed understanding of our embedded physiological responses is a good start towards understanding how our body reacts. We need to do this before trying to contain or constrain or get angry at our body for having those responses.

Serge: Okay. The feelings, the experiences, are bodily responses. We're in a process, and all life is interactive. Every living organism that has ever existed has responses to outside stimuli. We have these responses. Now, we're talking about the relationship we have with these responses.

Stephen: Yes. We want to complete the circle. That relationship has to be a respectful relationship. That's what I mean by stating that we need to respect our bodily responses. For me, respecting our bodily response is the basis for self-compassion.

Serge: We are an organism. And, like all living organisms, we have responses. These responses are just how we react to the external.

Are we functioning in such a way that we have respect for these responses? And do they provide a useful guide for action? Or are we at war against them, repressing them, not in touch with them, disrespecting them, ashamed of them?

Stephen: Do our bodily reactions hijack us? Our bodily state drives our behavior. Since we seldom track our bodily state and bodily reactions, we may not anticipate our shifts in vulnerabilities. Because we haven't attended to our body reactions, we do not anticipate the degree that bodily reactions can disrupt us.

Instead of developing better skills to monitor our shifts in state, we develop more elaborate narratives to justify how we direct our responses.

If we were in a mobilized state that results in a low threshold to become aggressive, we spontaneously generate a personal narrative that our reactions are justified. Someone has done something to us, and we need to get back at that person. The physiological mobilization hijacks our perspective of the world.

Serge: Right. So the evolutionary purpose of these responses is to help us orient. Through trauma or any other form of disconnection, the response is hijacked into the opposite of a helpful response. We are disoriented, and we create an orientation to something that is not reality.

Stephen: Our nervous system reacts as if these cues are cues of threat. We don't see it as an opportunity to co-regulate. We see this as a threat, which elicits a more primitive survival-oriented response.

Serge: It's interesting because I often use the concept of Sunflower Mind. As we're talking, this feels very similar to that sense of orienting. The sunflower orients to the sun, but imagine some big magnet that would pull the sunflower away from the sun. In the orientation with the sun, there is a sense of a dance, or a sense of co-regulation, of finding the right place of orienting. What you're talking about is being hijacked instead of being able to be in the dance.

Stephen: Your metaphor is really good because as the sunflower grows towards the sun, the sunflower thrives. It's going to absorb the energy from the sun to support growth. Metaphorically this is the opposite of what happens to humans when their physiological state hijacks their personal narrative. It disrupts their ability to co-regulate with another and co-regulation - metaphorically like the sun to a human being.

Serge: It feels very right. There is something very powerful about the word "co-regulation." Wouldn't it be interesting if we went through life thinking more in terms of co-regulation? What if we think about what we do in these terms instead of self-regulation? Instead of adapting? Instead of arguing? Are we striving to find the right way to co-regulate?

Stephen: I think our quest is really for safety. Co-regulation is our typical mechanism to obtain and experience safety. It enables our body to be calm. Remember, we're dealing with bodily responses, and our use of language is superimposed on our bodily reactions. Our body needs to be co-regulated. We can't do it on our own.

Serge: I want to highlight this. You're talking about "safety" as "co-regulation." From a threat model, we often think of safety as the absence of interaction. I'm going to withdraw. I'm going into my little corner, curling into a little ball, because that's where I have safety. It's very powerful when you talk about "safety as co-regulation".

Stephen: I do not see safety as the removal of threat.

Serge: Of course.

Stephen: Safety is something added. It's a special missing ingredient. Safety cues are face-to-face interactions, vocalizations, intonation of voice, prosody, gesture, proximity, cuddling. Since our body knows what cues signal safety, removing threats doesn't make us feel safe. Having people walk around with guns isn't making the environment safe unless the people have safety cues. This includes emotionally expressive upper faces with smiles, voices with melodic intonation, and appropriate gestures. We have to think about what we're doing as a society when we focus on removing threats and assuming that is sufficient to create feelings of safety.

Serge: I think that, maybe, the temptation to go to removal of threat comes from a place in the spectrum of trauma: "I've been hurt, and therefore I see safety as lack of interaction, as withdrawing, as withholding." The very, very powerful thing that you're emphasizing is that we need to educate ourselves that, as human beings, our nature is to find safety in interaction. As living beings, we can only find safety in interaction.

Stephen: Yes. I think that summarizes it beautifully.

Resources

The Proactive Twelve Steps and a discussion of each step are freely available to all at proactive12steps.com

The site features a list of related resources that is regularly updated: http://proactive12steps.com/resources

About

The author

Serge Prengel is in private practice and a co-founder of the *Integrative Focusing Therapy* online training program. He has been exploring creative approaches to mindfulness: how to live with an embodied sense of meaning and purpose.

He is the author of *Bedtime Stories For Your Inner Child* and co-editor of *Defining Moments For Therapists*.

The publisher

The Active Pause newsletter includes podcast conversations about mindfulness and what sustains us, articles, and upcoming events. Subscribe at http://activepause.com/newsletter

See other Active Pause books at: http://activepause.com/books

Endorsements of *The Proactive Twelve Steps*

(in alphabetical order)

This innovative revisioning of the Twelve Steps program gives the reader a practical, time-proven structure for making important life changes. Prengel's extensive clinical experience is reflected in his compassionate voice and the clarity of his guidance.

Judith Blackstone, PhD,
Author, *Trauma and the Unbound Body* and *Belonging Here*

11 years ago, I decided to get sober, and as I am not a religious person, I could not get to grips with the AA 12 steps or the big book, and it was your version of the 12 steps (proactive 12 steps) that saved me. If I didn't have yours to follow, I would have probably just thrown the AA book and refused to read it and still be an alcoholic to this day. So my words are here to you, sir, thanking you for giving me back my life, my children and helping me be brave enough to escape an abusive marriage. Stay safe and well. Thank you for my new life.

Miss Emma Marnie Burchill

In this book Serge Prengel not only harnesses the power of a traditional 12-step model but offers a broader non-religious prescriptive path for healing and change that goes beyond addressing addictive behaviors. The book's structure supports experiential self-inquiry to increase awareness, an essential component of the change process. It offers an in-depth perspective and specific instruction useful for those engaged in their own healing journey, as well as for professionals facilitating this process for others. After reading this book I immediately began to think of patients in my own practice to whom I would recommend it!

Eva Gold, PsyD, Author,
Buddhist Psychology and Gestalt Therapy Integrated: Psychotherapy for the 21st Century

12-Step programs can be of help, but the steps were originally cast in religious terms that can make it harder for believers and non-believers alike to see clearly the psychological skills that reside inside the steps. When that veil is lifted, it may be easier to create a safe place to face your fears without shut-down, fighting, or fleeing. This clear and well-written book presents a road to recovery in more modern, process-based terms that is, on the one hand, deeply resonant with 12-step traditions and, on the other, a fresh and uplifting reworking of the 12-step model. Definitely worth exploring.

Steven C. Hayes, PhD,
Foundation Professor of Psychology,
University of Nevada, Reno.
Originator and co-developer of
Acceptance and Commitment Therapy

Serge Prengel's "The Proactive Twelve Steps" is an alternative pathway to traditional twelve-step programs. It is infused with a sense of lightness of being which provides safe company to ourselves and others as we traverse the road to meaningful change. Compassionate and supportive, this new approach offers mindful ways to disentangle ourselves from our addictive patterns without shame or judgment. It is a kind and gentle way to step out of reactive patterns into presence and thus apply the principles of the Steps when needed. The Proactive Twelve Steps are a welcome gift to the world of recovery, offering healing to the body/mind/soul wounds that occur with addictive processes.

Suzanne Noel,
Founder, *Recovery Focusing*

This book invites both self-compassion and a deep dive into conversation with the self around the experiences of addiction, recovery, relapse, and healing, opening the door to including current understanding of the impact of stress and trauma on all of us as we struggle with being human.

Sarah Peyton, Author,
Your Resonant Self: Guided Meditations and Exercises to Engage Your Brain's Capacity for Healing

In *The Proactive Twelve Steps*, Serge Prengel reframes the 12-step model into an efficient manual for self-initiated change. The model brilliantly and succinctly provides a map to disentangle the individual from the pervasive constraints that have resulted in self-destructive behaviors, which have limited opportunities to enjoy life and to experience feelings of purpose and satisfaction. Through the sequential steps of the model, the devastating consequences of self-entanglement are deconstructed, leading to a greater sense of agency and a greater respect for opportunities to contribute to a benevolent 'ecosystem' in which sociality is expressed as mutual support and connectedness.

Stephen W. Porges, PhD,
Distinguished University Scientist, Kinsey Institute,
Indiana University Bloomington
Professor, Department of Psychiatry,
University of North Carolina at Chapel Hill

In this original, perceptive, and remarkable book, Serge Prengel has helped recovering people, clinicians, and, in fact, anyone interested in self-discovery. He has taken the insights of the Twelve-Step fellowships and has re-imagined them through the lenses of mindfulness and compassion in a way which is both profound and useful. In this book, Prengel has provided a meaningful roadmap for the recovery process, not just for those recovering from addictions but for all of us mortals. The book is both stimulating and practical and is an important milestone in the ongoing evolution of the Twelve Step fellowship. Its relevance for clinical practice and personal growth is unmistakable and important.

Mark Schenker, PhD,
Author, *A Clinician's Guide to 12-Step Recovery*

In *The Proactive Twelve Steps*, Prengel describes for readers how to go about making constructive choices one day at a time as well as moment by moment by applying a reflective, mindful orientation towards felt experience. This reformulation of the twelve-step method requires neither a therapist nor a life coach but is instead a self-help guide to finding and developing the power of choice. Each step is articulated in clear language, which does not require any higher power beyond the cultivation than one's own intuitive wisdom and compassion. In short, *The Proactive Twelve Steps* is a user-friendly guide to the application of mindfulness in everyday life.

Marjorie Schuman, PhD, Author,
*Inquiring Deeply: Mindfulness-Informed
Relational Psychotherapy and Psychoanalysis*

The Proactive Twelve Steps takes a mindful self-inquiry approach of self-discovery. Through this gradual understanding, people can make proactive choices to move from stuckness to transformation. I highly recommend this book to people in recovery as well as to anyone wishing to make proactive improvements in their lives.

Inge Sengelmann, LCSW, SEP, RYT, Author,
*It's Time to EAT: Embody, Awaken & Transform
our Relationship with Food, Body & Self*

You cannot live your best life unless you embrace your fears and vulnerabilities. *The Proactive Twelve Steps* show you how to do just that.

Kristen Ulmer,
Author, *The Art of Fear*

A sensible and sane take on behavior change, grounded in neuroscience. Prengel's objective is to take the powerful 12 steps of Alcoholic Anonymous and translate them into an accessible and secular-friendly program for change of all kinds. He is very realistic about what change actually entails, about the process of disentangling our addictions and stresses and coping strategies, and the role mindfulness has to play in all of it. This is a map of healing that can be used alongside personal and interpersonal practice. I was particularly moved by his descriptions of the healing power of community and compassionate listening. You can feel Prengel's own compassionate listening at work in these pages, a steady co-regulating presence that helps ground and orient the reader.

Jeff Warren,
Co-author, *Meditation for Fidgety Skeptics*

Serge Prengel's book offers a much-needed update of the Twelve Step tradition in addiction treatment. Trauma informed and neurobiologically based, it provides the reader with a sophisticated understanding of the nature of addiction. For those who are struggling with the limitations of the twelve steps this book can provide the best of an old tradition with a fresh, agnostic methodology. A must read.

Jan Winhall, MSW, FOT, Author,
*Treating Trauma and Addiction with
the Felt Sense Polyvagal Model*

Made in United States
North Haven, CT
21 February 2022